# Dreams, Visions and Revelations

## AND HOW TO INTERPRET THEM

By Dr. Peter Wyns

Dreams, Visions and Revelations & How to Interpret Them

To contact the author, please write to the below postal or email address:

Christians For Messiah Ministries
PO Box 36324
Rock Hill, SC 29732
Email: wynsusa@comporium.net

All scriptures taken from the New International Version unless otherwise noted.

Scriptures taken from the Holy Bible, New International Version ©

First Great Reward Publishing edition published 2022

Cover Design by: Rebecca Barrett

Editing by: Emma Donnelly, Joy Wyns, Jesse Enns, Cristal Donnelly and Bethany Ritter

Manufactured in the United States of America by Ingram Spark

ISBN: 978-1-7361159-3-0

$14.95

# Contents

Contents

**Part Two**
**Seven Kinds Of Dreams**

**Part Three**
**Remembering, Interpreting,**
**And Responding to Dreams**

# Contents

I am glad to dedicate this book to the members of Antioch International Church (AIC), and to those who connect with us through Christians for Messiah Ministries (CFM). Their hunger for more of God is inspiring. So many have become dear friends, and their fellowship is a great strength to Joy and me. They have partnered and assisted us in the work of the ministry, and without them we could not do all that the Lord has asked of us.

It is these dear friends who encouraged me to write this book. Besides asking me to write it, they confided in me by sharing many of their dreams along the way. Over time, they have told me that they are now able to interpret most of their own dreams without assistance. To hear these results is so beneficial. Without their encouragement and steadfastness, I do not think I would have written this book. Thank you, Antioch and CFM.

# Introduction

## Everyone, Everywhere

Whether they are high-tech or developing nations, all civilizations focus on dreams. Dreams are part of the make-up of every human soul and every soulish animal. Yes, even dogs and horses dream. This is observed by seeing rapid eye movement (REM) during sleep. Our physical bodies receive healing while we sleep, but so do our minds and souls. Dreams are part of a healing process to help facilitate a healthy mind. I believe it is the reason why soulish animals dream; it is a necessary ingredient for maintaining mental health.

As a side note, soulish animals are called nephesh in Hebrew. Although they are very limited when we compare them to humans, they still have a mind, will and emotions. They demonstrate care, compassion and even heroism. They can be trained by people to perform amazing feats as well as bringing pleasure and companionship.

Concerning humans, some groups give more credence to dreams and visions for direction and guidance than anything else. They believe dreams connect them to a spiritual world where secret truths are revealed. Many people do not remember their dreams and thus believe they do not dream, but all people dream. If believers understood their dreams they would discover that they are therapeutic and informative.

## For Christians

I would like to qualify that last statement because some folks have horrible dreams, and fear going to bed because of the trauma they might face in the night. That trauma is often associated with their daytime involvement with demonic activities and a sinful lifestyle. However, it may be the result of things from their past, or their ancestry that still need to be expunged from their lives. As Christians, we understand that God can speak to anyone at any time. This book has been written for Christians and some details will not apply to non-believers. I trust you have pleasant dreams. They, however, are for more than just night-time entertainment, although I must admit, some of my dreams have told such great stories, that I did not want to wake. At some level, nevertheless, a disciple's dream is always purposeful.

For non-Christians, there is no assurance that their dreams come from God. They might be demonic in origin.

## Fishing Dreams

Every day, fellow believers ask me to interpret their dreams. They know their dreams are meaningful, but they have not discovered how to interpret them. Others tell me their dreams and their interpretations, and I often think that their interpretations are incorrect and potentially harmful.

I still remember a teaching dream from when I was a teen. I had an opportunity to witness to someone about Christ, but I did not step up and obey the Lord. Later that night, I dreamt I was walking along the street with a fishing rod and tackle box in my hand. Then, a needy man slipped away without me helping him and telling him about Christ's love and care. Even though I had the equipment with me, I was not fishing. When I woke up, I knew the dream was connected to the man I failed the day before. I repented of my sin, because if anyone is given the opportunity to do good and doesn't do it, it is sin. *"If anyone, then, knows the good they ought to do and doesn't do it, it is a sin for them." Js.4:17*

Although I have not responded perfectly to that teaching dream, I am constantly reminded of it, even fifty years later.

Many years went by and I had another dream about fishing. I was fishing in a fast moving creek behind a house, when suddenly, my grandfather, Derek Prince, came out of the house and approached me. He took my rod in his hands, put a new worm on the hook and said, "Let me show you how to fish." He cast the line into the water and I woke up. I do not know if Grandpa Derek ever went fishing in his entire life, or if he even knew how to put a worm on a hook, but he was a great minister of the Gospel and he was my mentor. Every step along the way, the Lord has guided me forward by speaking to me in my dreams.

I have studied dreams and taught on the subject since I was young, yet it has taken more than fifty years to finally write a book on the subject. I hesitated for so long because there are so many factors to consider regarding dreams, and I do not want to mislead people with overly simplistic answers. With all I have gathered, I am now confident that I can help many Christians interpret their dreams. I trust you will enjoy my study and that it will be helpful and informative for you.

# PART ONE

# Everybody Dreams

# CHAPTER ONE

# Crazy Dreams

## They Had a Dream

"Sir, can you help me? I had a crazy, ridiculous dream. I am sure it doesn't mean anything but please tell me if there is anything to it."

That is how it usually begins. What seems like silly, disconnected images to the dreamer, are usually a very clear message once the riddle is solved. Dreams are so common, but so puzzling, that most folks have learned not to pay too much attention to them. They say, "It was just a dream!"

Others tell me they never dream, so they tend to discredit any hint of significance relegated to them. Some people believe that dreams might have a medical benefit, perhaps helping realign one's soul as part of a healthy sleep restoration pattern.

Still, others remain fixated by their dreams. Whether they are religious or not, they believe their dreams hold important messages for their lives. They believe that subliminal messages, and even future events, are captured in their dreams. Paul McCartney, the famous Beatles' singer and songwriter, says he received the entire melody for his song "Yesterday," one night in a dream (See his biography – "Many Years From Now", 1998, Barry Miles).

People wrestle to unlock the mysteries of their dreams. They share them with friends and colleagues as they search for answers. Usually, only guess work or inadequate suggestions follow. The dreams, though haunting, are mostly put on the shelf and forgotten over time. But, many so called crazy dreams are replayed in their minds and the obscure message is revisited.

## Dream Purpose

The purpose of dreams is so involved that I cannot delve deeply into it so early in the book. Although, at this time we will not focus on purpose, I want to highlight it briefly, so you will not miss something of great importance. If you do not read the entire book, I suggest you read chapter eighteen about God's plan to disciple you through dream encounters. A full and complete discipleship course is given to disciples through their dreams, but first they need to understand the process. Do not miss chapter eighteen. It makes all the difference.

## Scientific Analysis

Over the years, hundreds of research teams have set out to study sleep disorders, stages of sleep, and when people dream. Electronic impulse probes can measure the depth and intensity of one's sleep cycles, and when their brain impulses are most active. They determine when we are dreaming and plot graphs to understand sleep patterns. These, calculations reveal five major levels of healthy sleep and can suggest why some people say they do not dream. Really, they do dream, but only during certain stages of sleep, far from the moment they wake. They simply do not remember the dreams they have.

Regardless of the technical timing of dreams or the patterns of people's sleep, this book is focused on the messages and spiritual purpose of dreams. To me, dreams are not crazy or random, but important, purposeful and extremely instructive.

## Crazy Dreams I Avoid

My goal is to help good people understand their dreams. Dreams are helpful, even when they seem common-place, crazy or bizarre. Certain dreams, however, are crazy because they have been influenced by impure activity, the use of hallucinatory drugs, watching horror movies, or practicing sorcery or witchcraft. People who do such things open their souls to demonic entities that can interfere with their dreams. I usually avoid interpreting those dreams. Jesus came to heal and deliver people and we often help them, but I do not interpret their dreams because they could be controlled or influenced by evil spirits. Demons are deceivers, liars and destroyers. When they influence one's dream world, nothing they insert can be trusted.

People seeking to hear from God should renounce evil and receive Jesus Christ as their Savior and Lord. He will begin to speak to them in their dreams in order to heal and deliver them, through the power of the Holy Spirit.

## God Reaches Far

From time to time, I do interpret dreams for non-believers, if I feel that God is reaching out to them. He often comes to sinners in their dreams if they are searching for truth. I have known many ministers around the world who met the Lord through a dream or vision before any human spoke to them about Christ.

Recently, many such testimonies are coming out of Muslim nations such as Iran. Countless individuals have told of Jesus appearing to them in their dreams. These encounters have led to secret conversions of thousands of Muslims.

Jesus or an angel, appearing in the dreams of sinners is so powerful and many never hear of

Jesus before meeting Him in a dream. Angelic visitations through dreams and visions may be the only way that some people will ever hear of Christ. Scripture records, *"Then I saw another angel flying in midair, and <u>he had the eternal gospel to proclaim</u> to those who live on the earth-to every nation, tribe, language and people." Rev. 14:6* [Emphasis mine]

Do not be surprised if people from Muslim nations appear in your dreams. The Lord will show you them so you may pray for their salvation. Then, He will reach out to them in answer to your prayers.

## Unfamiliar Details

I am often amazed at what shows up in my dreams. Things I have never seen, places I have never been, and people I have never known end up in my dreams. Some, may think that dreams are the remembrances of things people see in life or on TV. No doubt, that is often true, but the surprise comes when things appear in dreams that are totally new to our experience. For example, people receive information in dreams in fields of science, of which they had no previous knowledge.

Einstein received dreams that helped him solve his 1905 theory of relativity (Mendiam, 2003). Einstein's contemporary, Niels Bohr gained insight into how electrons remain in their orbits, from a dream. Ottis Loewi, in 1921 had the same dream, on two separate nights, where he received information that led to his discovery of the chemical transmission of nervous impulse and he was able to conclusively prove it. (Loewi 1953) All of them received the Nobel Prize for these dream related discoveries. *Taken from the article – Sleep on a Problem... It works like a dream - by Josephine Ross – Google online.*

These and many other individuals were introduced to things for the first time in their dreams, and it gave them the answers they needed for complicated scientific solutions.

## Cartagena

When preaching on the subject of prayer in Cartagena, Colombia, I told the people that someone must have prayed for Nineveh to influence the hand of God to send Jonah there, so that revival could come. I asked, "Could it not happen here in Cartagena?" After lunch, I changed my teaching subject to dreams. After a couple of hours of teaching, I invited people to come forward and share their dreams. Then, I interpreted them in front of the congregation. During the service a lady stood to her feet. She introduced herself as the assistant to the city's mayor and had only come to the meetings, after lunch, for the first time. She said she had a dream the night before that made no sense to her. She heard a word in her dream that she had never heard before. It was crazy to her and she had no idea what it meant. She heard the word, "Nineveh". The lady was further surprised as she witnessed the room erupt with shouts of praise and amazement. We explained to her that I just preached about Nineveh that morning and compared it to Cartagena. The next day, she brought us a key to the city of Cartagena from the mayor's office. God had spoken to her in her dream. She received a word that she had never heard before. It was a sign to her, the mayor, and the believers who were present at the conference that if they pray, God would hear and answer with blessings for their city.

# CHAPTER TWO

# Dreams in the Bible

## Eight Ways to Hear God

The Bible teaches eight ways that we can hear the voice of God. He will speak to us:

1. Through the Scriptures
2. Through His Spirit within us
3. Through angels
4. Through dreams and visions
5. Through an audible voice

6. Through other people such as ministers
7. Through signs and wonders
8. Through God-ordained circumstances

When you have important decisions to make you need to hear from God in two or three of these ways to be sure you are following His direction.

Among the ways God speaks to us, we discover dreams and visions. They are so common in the Bible that over two hundred verses focus on the theme. Every notable person in the Bible had a dream or vision from God and they were all dreams of importance. Their dreams became part of the story of their significance and greatness. God spoke to His people through dreams then and this pattern has only increased today.

## God Speaks through Dreams

God spoke to many men and women in the Bible through dreams and visions.

- Enoch
- Abraham
- Abimelek

- Joseph
- Jacob
- Pharaoh
- The butler
- The baker
- Elijah
- Daniel
- Nebuchadnezzar
- Ezekiel
- Jeremiah
- Hosea
- Joel
- Isaiah
- Solomon
- Saul
- Zechariah
- Joseph (Mary's husband)
- The Wise Men
- Pilate's wife
- Peter
- Paul
- John
- Jesus

This is by no means a complete list but it shows us how often God uses dreams and visions to speak to His people.

Every dream in the Bible comes from God, even the ones that sinners had. For example, Abimelek, Pharaoh, Nebuchadnezzar and Pilate's wife all had dreams from God, even though they did not worship or submit their lives to Him. I am not suggesting that all dreams that sinners have come from God. In fact, I think that most of them do not because, as previously stated, ungodly people open doors for demons to enter and give those entities access to their souls and minds. Evil spirits can orchestrate dreams to influence and deceive.

I am sure that not all dreams that sinners have are demonic. In our minds, it is possible to hear three different voices: God's voice, the voice of an evil spirit, or the voice of our own soul (which is also called our flesh). Those who have not surrendered their lives to Christ can have dreams that come from any of these sources. They can come from God, demons, or from one's own soul life. God's people, on the other hand, have dreams only from God, if they walk with the Lord. No believer in the Bible received a dream that God did not give them. Even dreams of terror are credited to come from God, in order for warnings and flushing to occur (see Job 33:15).

## How God Speaks

God called Moses, Aaron and Miriam to stand before Him as He gave ominous instructions and counsel to them. In an audible voice, He reaffirmed Moses' leadership, but in His pre-amble, He told them how He speaks to His prophets. *"When a prophet of the Lord is among you, I reveal myself to him in visions, I speak to him in dreams." Num. 12:6*

God chose the vehicle of dreams and visions to speak to His servants. This was one of the main ways He communicated His Word back in the Old Testament, and it has only increased under the New Covenant.

## Pentecostal Dreams

The Lord emphasized the importance of dreams and visions on the day of Pentecost when he inspired Peter to quote from the words of the prophet Joel. Peter said, *"In the last days, God says, I will pour out my Spirit on all people. Your sons and your daughters will prophesy, your young men will see visions, your old men will dream dreams. Even on my servants, both men and women, I will pour out my Spirit and they will prophesy." Acts 2:17-18*

The outpouring of the Holy Spirit marks the birth of the Church. Instead of the Holy Spirit coming only to a select group of Old Testament prophets and patriarchs, in the New Testament, we discover that He comes to all people who repent and are baptized.

As mentioned in the above verse, the key signs that accompany the Holy Spirit's impartation; are gifts of prophesy, dreams and visions. Dreams and visions are not relegated to Old Testament patriarchs, but they are brought to a new level of importance for all believers who receive the Holy Spirit under the New Covenant. Later, in the Scriptures, we discover that another sign associated with the outpouring of the Holy Spirit was added: speaking in tongues. *"While Peter was still speaking these words, the Holy Spirit came on all who heard the message. The circumcised believers who had come with Peter were astonished that the gift of the Holy Spirit had been poured out even on the Gentiles.*

*For they heard them speaking in tongues and praising God." Acts 10:44-46*

## Don't Dismiss God's Plan

Regardless of our doctrine, preferences, or different ideas, all true disciples listen and obey the Lord. We believe there is no stronger voice of God in our lives than the directives that come from the New Testament Scriptures. That means we cannot dismiss dreams and visions as being unimportant or insignificant. They are an integral manifestation of the outpouring of the Holy Spirit and a common occurrence for God's people throughout the New Testament. Starting with Joseph, the husband of Mary, four dreams were given to guide him forward with his responsibilities to take Mary as his wife, and protect baby Jesus. The Magi were warned in a dream of Herod's treachery, so they returned home by a different route. Even Jesus was given several visions. For example, He had a vision of Satan falling like lightning and of Nathaniel sitting under a fig tree. Peter had a vision of a sheet full of unclean animals being lowered before his eyes.

Paul had a dream of a Macedonian man calling for help and John had a vision; it is the entire book of Revelation.

## Get Ready Church

The Church must get ready to experience a new level of supernatural partnership with God. It cannot complete His end-time purpose by relying on man's wisdom alone. We will discover increased power and miraculous signs and wonders will go before us. Much of it will come to us through dreams and visions. Ask the Lord to speak to you in the night as well as during the day. Let the 24 hour cycle of your spiritual walk be complete.

# CHAPTER THREE

# Power Dreams

## Casual Dreams

Many people have several dreams every night. If they tried to interpret every detail from all of their dreams, they would do little else in life. It would become so consuming that the focus of their lives would be totally off balance. I suggest that dreamers learn to determine the dreams which are most important and concentrate on them, while paying little attention to the rest of their dreams. Dreams that are not so dynamic I call "casual dreams".

Pray for people in your casual dreams. Receive the simple message that God is showing you and respond with thanksgiving, renunciation, rebuke, or intercessory prayer as you feel you should. Then leave them behind, unless the Lord continues to remind you of them. After responding to them appropriately, put them on the shelf and go on with your life. In the final chapters of the book we will discuss appropriate responses to dreams.

## Power Dreams

I call the important dreams, "power dreams". These stay with you for days, or months and sometimes years. When you have a power dream, you wake up deeply impacted by what you witnessed. When individuals in the Bible had power dreams they woke up exhausted, and so impacted that they were emotionally driven to find the interpretation of them.

Pharaoh had multiple power dreams. He called his wise men to find the answers to the riddles of his dreams. One was about fourteen cows and the other was about fourteen sheaves of wheat. *"In the morning his mind was troubled, so he sent for all the magicians and wise men in*

*Egypt. Pharaoh told them his dreams, but no one could interpret them for him." Gen. 41:8*

Nebuchadnezzar also had a power dream. He was so impacted by it that he threatened to kill all of the wise men who served him if they could not tell him the meaning of his dream. *The king replied to his astrologers, "This is what I have firmly decided: If you do not tell me what my dream was and interpret it, I will have you cut into pieces and your houses turned into piles of rubble." Dan. 2:5*

Some dreams, whether good or bad, are so gripping that the dreamer has to find out what they mean. Those are power dreams. Those are the ones I suggest you focus on, discover what they mean, and respond appropriately. They are important.

## Dreams that Repeat

There are other dreams, besides power dreams, that you should pay close attention to. They are the ones that are repeated three or more times. When this happens, God is trying to tell you something that is very important. Pay close attention to those dreams and do not ignore them. They may not feel like power dreams but they carry a message of importance that requires your response. When a dream is repeated you should go on a journey to discover what the Lord is telling you. Is He leading you to break off curses, find healing for your body or soul, or connect with a specific calling or purpose for your life? If so, respond with the appropriate action or activity to deal with the matter.

## Cancer in My Dreams

Three times within ten days I had the same dream. I dreamt that a doctor, nurse and healthcare worker came to me in different dreams, but all of them brought me the same message: I had cancer.

Following the very first dream, I prayed against, and rebuked the spirit of cancer when I woke. However, I did not feel I won the battle. It seemed like my prayers were not effective and the dream kept returning. I soon became frustrated.

Several events occurred during this time period, and later I realized, they were connected. A person was attending our Church who was anti-Semitic. Even though I am Jewish, he continued to attend our services and often heard me preach positive messages of God's blessings for Israel. I had several breakfast appointments with him to help him understand the Scriptures, but I was not successful. He was an artist and I bought a beautiful painting from him and hung it in my home. Then one day, my son-in-law pointed out some hidden words in the corner of the painting: "Jews Must Die." We were shocked.

During the same season a friend, who is a medical doctor, pointed out that I had a small growth in my ear. He suspected it was cancer.

When I received the third dream telling me that I had cancer, I woke in sweat and panic. In the middle of the night, I desperately called upon the Lord, and he gave me the scripture about the prophet Ehud thrusting a knife into the body of a wicked king named Eglon (see Judges 12). As I read the scripture, I felt the power of God come upon me. I rose up, and with authority, I rebuked the spirit of cancer that was attacking me. This time I felt it leave and I received victory. I believe the painting carried a curse and I brought it into my home.

After discovering its wicked, subliminal message, I took the painting off the wall, went out into the back garden and burned it: frame and all.

The three repeated dreams and the cancerous attack against me happened more than seven years ago. I have had no signs of cancer in my body, before or since then. I have had routine checkups with my doctor since then and I have no cancer.

Concerning the problem inside my ear, I anointed it with oil and prayed over it every day. Within a month the mole that was growing there, fell out. To his surprise, my doctor friend verified that it was completely gone, when I visited him a few months later.

## Informative Dreams

Last night I had a few dreams. They were not power dreams, but they were informative. In one of them, I was told that our church was hosting three different funerals in one day and one of them involved a senior in his nineties. Also in the dream, two of my family members were visiting, and I was talking with them.

Although these were casual dreams, they were informative. When I woke, I prayed for the people and families in my dreams. I also prayed for those members of my family. I postured myself to be ready to serve those families, and not be surprised when these events occur. I realized that many people in the Church would have to help, when such events happen and I began to think of the logistics and preparations needed for such a time. I did not know most of the guests who were attending those three funerals. Hundreds of people were in the dreams. I have no doubt that such a time will come one day and when it does the Church will be ready to serve. The Lord is preparing us to care for His people and that is why He gave me these dreams. These are casual dreams but they are informative. I have dreams like this almost every night. I am thankful for them because they help prepare me for what is coming and often show me the situation I am facing right now. I process casual dreams within a few minutes after waking, as I prepare for the day ahead of me. I pray, think things through, and sometimes I respond by making a couple of phone calls. Then, I put those casual dreams on the shelf, and go on with other matters of life and ministry. I am so thankful. I realize that God is always going ahead of me.

# CHAPTER FOUR

# Dreams, Visions and Revelations

## Dreams, Visions and Revelations

Much confusion occurs in the Church because many people do not understand the basic difference between dreams, visions and revelations. When we fail to recognize their individual dynamics, we give each the same level of authority and that can lead to misdiagnosis and error. The Bible teaches and gives examples of each and indicates how they differ. Understanding how they functions would solve many prophetic problems that are present in the Church today.

## Dreams

Dreams are personal stories, accompanied by words and impressions that we receive when we are sleeping. This is so important for believers, because God wants to speak to us in the night as much as He does during the day. When we are sleeping, He has our undivided attention. We are not involved with the care of our children, work assignments, or other matters of life. God has an open channel to us without the involvement or business of others. In the Bible dreams are sometimes called night visions.

Dreams are involuntary. We never know what will come to us in our dreams. We have no ability to self-design, control the subject matter, or fashion the details of what will be shown to us. Having peace with God, however, is essential if we want to receive pure messages that bring God's intended benefits through dreams. Once we recognize the importance of our dreams and begin to seek the Lord regarding this doorway of communication, the Lord will increase the frequency. The more we learn the voice of God through dreams, the more trusted we will be with messages of greater significance and importance.

Our dream journey is designed to activate the prophetic gift the Lord intends for us. Prophecy is the ability to hear from God and then share what He gives with others. As we discovered in an earlier chapter, the message of Pentecost showed us that dreams, visions and prophecy are connected. A Christian who dreams a lot has a prophetic calling and should learn how to accurately interpret what the Lord is giving them. *"When a prophet of the Lord is among you, I reveal myself to him in visions, I speak to him in dreams." Num. 12:6*

## Visions

Visions are not the same as revelations. Many people say they had a vision when really they had a revelation. Revelations must be judged like prophecy, because they could just be our own ideas. Visions, on the other hand, are much more powerful; they involve us going into a trance. I have personally experienced a few of these in my life.

A vision is not an idea or a picture that some-one has in their mind's eye, but is a movie that is actually seen, similar to a dream. Something appears before them and they enter a spiritual dimension. *"Peter went up on the roof to pray. He became hungry and wanted something to eat, and while the meal was being prepared, he fell into a trance. He saw heaven opened and some-thing like a large sheet being let down to the earth by its four corners. It contained all kinds of four-footed animals, as well as reptiles of the earth and birds of the air. Then a voice told him, 'Get up, Peter. Kill and eat.'" Acts 10:9-13*

Later, we discover that Peter calls what he saw in the trance, a vision. *"While Peter was wondering about the meaning of the vision, the men sent by Cornelius found out where Simon's house was and stopped at the gate." Acts 10:17*

## Paul's Vision

A similar thing happened to Saul, whom we know as Paul. *"As he neared Damascus on his journey, suddenly a light from heaven flashed around him. He fell to the ground and heard a voice say to him, "Saul, Saul, why do you perse-cute me?" "Who are you, Lord?" Saul asked. "I am Jesus whom you are persecuting." He replied. "Now get up and go into the city and you will be told what you must do." Acts 9:3-6*

Saul's companions heard the sounds and light but did not see what Saul saw. Saul was blinded by the encounter and could not see for the next three days. This was not just an idea that he had in his head. Later, while talking with King Agrippa, he identified this experience as a heavenly vision. He said, *"So then King Agrippa, I was not disobedient to the vision from heaven." Acts 26:19*

Visions, like dreams, are actual things that you see, often with spoken words that you hear. When someone falls into a trance and has a vision, it is so powerful that they never forget it. It is so impactful and definitive that they adjust their lives to obey the vision they received. Visions carry enormous weight and authority and should not be confused with revelations.

## John Babu

Jesus appeared in a vision to my good friend, John Babu, while he was still a Hindu. John was dying of liver cancer and went into a Hindu temple, in India, to pray to his gods. Suddenly,

Jesus appeared to him and told him to stop worshipping false gods. John ran outside and sat on the bench, under a tree in front of the temple. While he was wondering what had just happened, he fell into another trance and Jesus appeared to Him a second time. He had never heard of Jesus before, but through this encounter, John was converted and later became a great disciple. With training, he became a powerful minister of the Gospel, leading more than seven thousand Hindu's to Christ and extending oversight and care to more than one hundred churches.

## Revelations

Revelations are also from God, but they do not carry the same authority as dreams or visions. That is why, when someone has a revelation, they should not say they had a vision.

We read, *"What then shall we say, brothers? When you come together, everyone has a hymn, or a word of instruction, a revelation, a tongue or an interpretation. All of these must be done for the strengthening of the church." 1Cor. 14:26*

In this verse we read about a revelation. It is a thought or picture in one's mind's eye. Like a prophetic word, it should come from God and be given for edification and strengthening of the Church, but it is not a vision.

Someone could say, "I saw a vision of hundreds of angels filling the room and releasing explosions of fire over the congregation." Perhaps this was not a vision at all but a revelation. In other words, it may be something the person pictured and it could have come from God. On the other hand, it might be an emotional picture but not an actual truth from God. It is possible, that there are not hundreds of angels present; releasing fire. People may receive it as a true revelation from God and their faith may increase but it should be put on the shelf and tested like any other prophetic word. Unless the prophet went into a trance and actually saw physical angels and real fire, they did not have a vision, they had a revelation.

## Dreams, Visions and Revelations

If we have a dream, we can say, "I saw or heard something in a dream". Then, a correct interpretation can be of great benefit.

If we fall into a trance and God shows us a vision, we should describe it as such. Then, we should judge the minister who is sharing it with us to determine its accuracy. We should know those who labor among us so we can be sure of their honesty and integrity. A true heavenly vision carries immense authority and should be received with great care and follow-through obedience.

If we have a revelation, we should say so and not call it a vision. It should then be judged to determine if it is a true word from God. We handle a revelation in the same way we handle all prophetic words. If it is found to be true, it will give us guidance and resolve.

# CHAPTER FIVE

# The Obvious, the Riddle, the Impossible

## A Deeper Dream Purpose

The Holy Spirit will orchestrate dreams to accomplish His purpose in the life of an individual.

1. Dreams may be obvious. God may simply communicate clear messages with His sons or daughters while they are sleeping.

2. Dreams may be riddles. God may want someone to seek Him more fervently, so He gives that person a dream that requires them to search for an interpretation. That dream will involve a riddle that can be solved, but it will require some effort.

3. Dreams may also be impossible to understand without a supernatural gift of interpretation. Those dreams require a third party with whom God wants the dreamer to connect. This happened with Pharaoh who needed to connect with Joseph. It also happened to Nebuchadnezzar who needed to connect with Daniel. In both cases, the dream interpretation gift allowed Joseph and Daniel to be promoted to the position of Prime Minister of these nations.

## The Obvious

Dreams given to disciples are often obvious. They reveal a message from the Lord that does not require any additional help or special gift to understand. Here are some obvious messages given in dreams to Joseph, the husband of Mary: *"But after he had considered this, an angel of the Lord appeared to him in a dream and said, 'Joseph son of David, do not be afraid to take Mary home as your wife, because what is conceived in her is from the Holy Spirit.'"* Mt. 1:20

This dream gave Joseph an obvious message; it needed no deep interpretation. It happened again to Joseph after Jesus was born: *"When they had gone, an angel of the Lord appeared to Joseph in a dream. 'Get up,' he said, 'take the child and his mother and escape to Egypt. Stay there until I tell you, Herod is going to search for the child to kill him.' So he got up, took the child and his mother during the night and left for Egypt."* Mt. 2:13-14

The message in Joseph's dream was so obvious that when he woke, in the middle of the night, he immediately obeyed the word that the Lord had sent to him in his dream. If he had not obeyed the obvious message in the dream, the life of the Christ child would have remained in harm's way.

## The Riddle

The meaning of all dreams is not obvious. In fact, most are given to us in riddles: *"When a prophet of the Lord is among you, I reveal myself to him in visions, I speak to him in dreams. But this is not true of my servant Moses; he is faithful in all my house. With him I speak face to face, clearly and not in riddles..."* Num. 12:6-8

This Scripture teaches us that generally, God speaks to his prophets in riddles in their dreams. Once an individual discovers their dream language, it is fairly easy for them to solve the riddles and interpret their dreams.

One of the funniest dreams in the Bible was given to a Midianite guard whose fellow soldier interprets and Gideon overhears it. It is not an obvious message, but it is a riddle that is easily interpreted. In the dream, their tent is smashed by a loaf of bread rolling down upon them from the hills. They quickly solved the riddle of the dream and got the message that the Israelites would soon defeat them.

*"Gideon arrived just as a man was telling a friend his dream. 'I had a dream,' he was saying. 'A round loaf of barley bread came tumbling into the Midianite camp. It struck the tent with such force that the tent overturned and collapsed.' His friend responded, 'This can be nothing other than the sword of Gideon son of Joash, the Israelite.*

*God has given the Midianites and the whole camp into his hands.'" Jdg. 7:13-14*

The riddle was simple; their military tent was smashed and destroyed by a loaf of bread. They put the pieces together and solved the riddle. It was their tent. An enemy coming in the form of a round loaf of bread destroyed it, so the bread must be Gideon and the Israelites. Furthermore Gideon and his family were grain farmers (see Jdg.6:11). The Midianite army knew about Gideon, the grain farmer who was now leading the armies of Israel. The association between a loaf of bread crashing into their tent, and Gideon the grain farmer, was an easy connection to make. They solved the riddle of the dream and it is amazing, if not hilarious, that God orchestrated the timing so that Gideon was there at that precise moment to hear it.

## The Impossible

The third kind of dream is impossible to understand without supernatural help. In this case, God has to reveal the symbolism in the dream or people will just be guessing when they try to come up with an interpretation. Impossible dreams were not common in the Bible. However, they were often given to nonbelievers such as Pharaoh and Nebuchadnezzar who needed to be convinced of the presence of the Living God and the authority that rested on His servants, the prophets.

Nebuchadnezzar had a dream about a statue with a head of gold, a chest of silver, a belly of bronze, legs of iron and feet of iron and clay. Then a rock cut from a mountain smashed the entire statue and grew to fill the whole earth and stay forever. To make the encounter even more impossible, God caused Nebuchadnezzar to forget the dream. The king called all of his wise men together and demanded that they first tell him what the dream was and then interpret it. If they failed, they would be executed.

*"The astrologers answered the king, 'There is not a man on earth who can do what the king asks!'" Dan. 2:10*

Upon hearing their words, the king ordered all of them to be killed. When Daniel heard this, he asked for an opportunity to speak to the king. *"Then Daniel replied, 'No wise man, enchanter, magician, or diviner can explain to the king the mystery he has asked about, but there is a God in heaven who reveals mysteries. He has shown King Nebuchadnezzar what will happen in days to come.'" Dan. 2:27-28*

Then, Daniel proceeded to tell the king his dream and also what the dream meant. *"Then the king placed Daniel in a high position and lavished many gifts on him. He made him ruler over the entire province of Babylon and placed him in charge of all of its wise men." Dan. 2:48*

The dream God gave Nebuchadnezzar was about the entire history of humanity, from the reign of Nebuchadnezzar until the second coming of Christ and beyond. It would be impossible for Nebuchadnezzar and all of his wise men to correctly interpret this dream. Only by a supernatural gift of interpretation could it be understood.

## To God Be the Glory

Sometimes, God withholds a dream's interpretation so He will be glorified when His servant brings forth its meaning. Dreams are designed by God for both His momentary and His eternal purpose. Their messages are extremely important for His children, and His disciples should study to discover the hidden treasures within them.

Dreams may contain an obvious message, a hidden riddle that can be solved, or a message that requires a supernatural word of knowledge to interpret. Each one should be explored and we should be humbled and empowered by them.

# CHAPTER SIX

# Discovering Your Dream Language

## A Gift of Discernment

When a dreamer begins to appreciate their dreams, they can start to discover their dream language. People have their own dream language and once discovered, they can interpret most of their dreams with speed and accuracy. However, certain guidelines must be learned along the way to help avoid error, as accuracy is essential for dream students.

The most important element for interpreting a dream is to remember the emotion that was felt during different parts of a dream. I call this your dream discernment, because dream feelings are always accurate. When you feel something or someone is good in your dream, then they are good in life as well. You may be fooled in life but not in your dream. If someone or something is bad in your dream, then they may be bad in life as well. Always do your best to recognize your dream feelings and learn from them.

Discerning your feelings in your dreams is so important because a dog, for example, can be an attacker or your best friend. Your emotional feelings will tell you if the dog is a friend or an enemy, otherwise you can be led astray and accept a wrong interpretation for your dream.

This gift of dream discernment has another application. You will immediately know something in your dream even if the object is not exactly the same in real life. For example, your ancestral home may be different in the dream, yet you know the home in your dream still represents your ancestral home. Your church may look different, but it is still your church. People can look different, yet you know them and identify them as certain individuals. Your dream discernment is accurate, even when the physical identification is different. Trust your feelings and you will have dream discernment.

There is a third kind of discernment in your dreams. For example, you are given an immediate knowledge of something without any explanation or introduction. This is amazing. You may see someone for the first time in your dream, yet you know instinctively the details of their purpose or occupation. No one has to tell you, but you are aware, for example, that the person before you is a university professor who is an expert in archeology. They have authority and knowledge of that subject and you trust them as they begin to speak in your dream.

These three aspects of discernment will be present in your dreams:

1. Your emotions identify the evil or good that is present.
2. Your recognition of people or things even though they may look different in real life.
3. Your immediate knowledge of someone's back ground and purpose even though no one has told you.

These dynamics are not strange or unusual. They are part of the discernment gifts that God gives to help you navigate your sleep journey.

## Common Dream Symbols

To help you get started, I have listed some common symbols that will give you a head start for solving the riddles in your dreams. In the preceding paragraphs, I shared with you the importance of recognizing dream discernment. Emotional feelings should help you determine the validity of common symbols that may appear in your dreams. In other words, do not simply attach a good meaning to something because it may be frequently interpreted that way. Give it the "feelings" test first.

Here is my partial list of dream symbols to help you get started. This is what I have personally discovered after studying the subject for decades and interpreting thousands of dreams for people along the way. This list is by no means complete, but these are commonly occurring dream details:

**<u>The House You Grew Up In</u>** = The spiritual condition of your family or your life or the blessings or curses that are being passed down from your ancestry.

**A Vast Ocean** = The government of God

**A Violent Ocean** = The judgment of God or an demonic attack

**Dark Depths of Water** = A great foreboding danger

**An Evil Wolf** = An attacker that may run in a pack

**An Evil Bear** = A ruthless killer

**An Evil Dog** = An attacker sent to hurt

**A Good Dog** = A friend sent to help

**A Lion** = An evil that hunts

**A Good Lion** = A protection angel

**Birds Attacking** = Demons

**Good Ministers and Good People of Authority** = The counsel and covering of God

**Good Family Members** = The helpful guidance or comfort of God (Even if they are already deceased. It is not necromancy if it happens in your dreams)

**Good Angels** = Messengers from God to teach, protect, provide for, and direct you

**Jesus or God's Throne Room** = Will bring the overwhelming glory, presence and majesty of God

**A Calm River** = Peace and comfort

**A Rough River** = Trials and tribulations

**Driving In Your Car** = Your life journey

**In Another Person's Car** = Their life journey or mission (good or bad)

**Perverted Sexual Experience** = Temptation sent to bring you down

**An Invitation to be Corrupt** = Temptation sent to bring you down

**A Boat or Yacht** = A vessel taking you to God's purpose

**A Tree or Forest** = A person or a crowd of people

**Sunshine and Warmth** = God's blessings

**Lack of Appropriate Clothing** = An attack against your personal confidence

**Continually Being Ill Prepared** = An attack against your personal confidence

**Repeated Failure** = An attack against your personal confidence

**Natural Disasters in Dreams** = Judgments from God or a demonic attack

**Flying** = God's blessings to refresh and give you perspective

## Dream Language

This chapter will help you get started with the interpretation of your dreams. However, it is not everything you need to understand your dreams. Some dreams are complicated and require waiting on the Lord. Talking with God about your dreams is part of being a disciple. We should learn the correct questions to ask Him and listen to receive the answers. Learning about the seven types of dreams that the Bible speaks of will help us talk with the Lord and better understand His direction.

Our conversation with the Lord should be seamless. We go to bed talking with Him and wake up in conversation with Him as well. We talk with Him throughout the day and in the night, He continuously speaks to us.

# PART TWO

# Seven Kinds Of Dreams

# CHAPTER SEVEN

# Teaching Dreams

## Categorizing Your Dreams

I have discovered seven kinds of dreams in the Bible. They are as follows:

1. Teaching dreams
2. Provision dreams
3. Warning dreams
4. Flushing dreams
5. Apocalyptic dreams
6. Glory dreams
7. Destiny dreams

Once you understand these different kinds of dreams you will be better equipped to interpret them. If you receive a power dream, but it is complicated or mysterious, you should ask the Lord what kind of dream you had. It may be a teaching dream, but also a glory dream or a warning dream (at this same time).

Perhaps a bear was chasing you and you realize this was a warning. The next question is, "What am I being warned about? What does the bear represent?" You know you are under attack and it will be helpful to pinpoint who or what the attacker is, in order to take appropriate action. Likewise, if you recognize you just received a teaching dream, then you can ask, "Lord, what are you teaching me?" Isolating the kind of dream you had narrows down your search and gives you a specific category to investigate.

In the next few chapters I will explain the seven kinds of dreams and how they differ from each other, give examples from the Bible and present-day experiences. To start with we will investigate the teaching dream.

## Teaching Dreams

The Holy Spirit is both teacher and comforter. He has all knowledge and wisdom but the teaching involves more than just passing on information. He will change our way of thinking, our character, and our activities. This process is called *sanctification* and through it we become more Christ-like. The teaching of the Holy Spirit is called the wisdom from above; it is an impartation of character and knowledge.

If the Holy Spirit was just giving us information, His teaching would not require such intensity. But since it is a character-changing impartation, it requires intimate lessons that impact us. People who have learned to appreciate their dreams will sometimes discover that the Lord is teaching them more while they are sleeping, then when they are awake. A perfect example of this is found in the Bible.

## Solomon's Dream

*"At Gibeon the Lord appeared to Solomon during the night in a dream, and God said, Ask for whatever you want me to give you." 1Kgs. 3:5*

Immediately, we can categorize this as a glory dream because the Lord appeared in it. We also discover that it is a teaching dream. God's method of teaching in this dream is amazing. I think it demonstrates the best way to teach that has ever been recorded.

The dream starts off with a request; the Lord says, "Ask me what you want."

Then, God switches places and responds as if He is Solomon. In the dream, Solomon says, *"Now, O Lord my God, you have made your servant king in the place of my father David. But I am only a child and do not know how to carry out my duties. Your servant is here among the people you have chosen, a great people, too numerous to count or number. So give your servant a discerning heart* [wisdom] *to govern your people and to distinguish between right and wrong." 1Kgs. 3:7-9*

After showing Solomon His perfect answer, and causing him to say it with his own mouth, He switches back to speak as God and congratulate Solomon for a perfect response. We read, *"So God said to him, 'Since you have asked for this and not for long life or wealth for yourself, nor have you asked for the death of your enemies but for discernment in administering justice, I will do what you have asked. I will give you a wise and discerning heart...Moreover, I will give you what you have not asked for – both riches and honor – so that in your lifetime, you will have no equal among kings. And if you walk in my ways and obey my statutes and commands as David your father did, I will give you a long life.' Then Solomon awoke – and he realized it had been a dream."* 1Kgs. 3:11-15

## God Gave the Dream

We do not decide what we dream or determine the sequence of events in them. God gave Solomon a dream where He asked him to choose what he wanted. Then, in the dream, He has Solomon answer with godly wisdom and because he answered correctly, God gave him amazing blessings.

Solomon was watching this take place in his dream. He was taught; how to speak with God, what God expected of him, and what the results of obedience would bring.

Here are some of the details that God taught Solomon while he was sleeping:

1. Humility
2. Care for people
3. That the people of Israel are chosen and great
4. That he should not seek personal fame
5. That he should not seek riches
6. That he should not seek to kill his enemies
7. That he should seek wisdom to rule well
8. That blessings will follow godly behavior
9. That God loved his father David, and told Solomon to follow his example
10. That God would give more to His obedient children, than what they ask for

## My Teaching Dreams

I dream every night and most of them are teaching dreams. Some will teach me things I already know, but need to be reminded of. Some teaching dreams are power dreams and are so instructive that I learn things that I never knew before. The Lord has shown me the results of political elections, before the outcome was announced. He has also shown me what my focus should be so I might lead His people well.

## Election Night

During the night of the last election, the Lord gave me two dreams. In the first dream He showed me the outcome of the election and that the results would not be overturned.

In the second dream, I was asleep in bed and woke to see two black wolves in my room. This was still while I was dreaming. One was sitting on its haunches and the other lying beside it, motionless and almost dead. At first I was afraid, but then I realized they were there to receive help and not to hurt me.

Still in my dream, I went back into my bed and woke again. The wolves were still there, but this time, there was also a wounded deer in the room. He was bleeding and leaning against the wall. His blood was smearing against the wall as it slid toward my bed. I got up and tried to get it out of the room, because I did not want a bleeding deer in my bedroom. Then I woke up.

## The Teaching

I will not tell you everything the Lord taught me that night, but the essence of the teaching was that during the next season of preaching I should instruct the Church not to be political. The nation is polarized (wounded black wolves and a wounded white tailed deer), and this polarization exists among Christians. We need healing. The Lord showed me that both groups wanted to be in my room. So for the next season, I was to focus on healing and coming together.

Before the election, I was focused on the political climate in America and how Christians should vote responsibly. After the election, God taught me to shift my focus toward the healing of His Church. For the next six months my sermons focused on unity.

## Amazing Teachings

I think the most amazing teaching I received in my dreams, was when the Lord gave me an entire sermon for Sunday's service. It has happened two times in my life. On one of those occasions, the Lord gave me part of a sermon to preach. The other time, the Lord gave me a three point sermon with verses of scripture and illustrations to highlight the points. It was so complete that I simply had to write it down when I woke and preach it on Sunday.

## Status Quo Dreams

A sub-category of teaching dreams I call, "status quo dreams". They are casual dreams and carry less importance than others. Status quo dreams will often have so many awkward twists and turns, that at first, they are hard to understand. You might not realize what is happening, but God is revealing the status quo of your life and your surroundings. The dream depicts what is going on at this time. It includes many different things, so the dream seems to shift in all sorts of directions and the details seem disconnected.

A status quo dream tells you what others are thinking of you or where they are spiritually. It shows you what is taking place in your community or around the world. No matter what direction it takes, the story line seems disheveled. I remember, years ago, some newscasters would give a sixty-second, around the world, news overview. They would allot eight to ten seconds on each subject and cover seven or eight major topics in sixty seconds. A status quo dream is like that.

It will reveal the good, the bad, and the ugly. Sometimes the details are not very dynamic but other times a status quo dream may leave you feeling confused and heavy-hearted, especially if it reveals spiritual battles on the front lines where teachers, police officers, or pastors live.

This type of dream tells you that God knows where you live and what you are facing and that He understands the spiritual dynamics around you. It may reveal His burden for society or some situation and point to areas that need prayer.

Status quo dreams are often cryptic and symbolic. Here is an example of one that I had recently.

*'I found myself in a messy, basement room. I think it belonged to a ministry friend of mine, although I did not see his face. I also think he asked me to help him decorate the room so he could make a ministry presentation. He showed me what I could use but then I watched him cut the decorations into short pieces. I wanted to help*

*him so I began cleaning up the clutter but there was too much and I could not complete the task. Then I tried to use the material he had given me for decorating. It was in tiny pieces, there was so little of it and it was awful looking. It looked like homemade Lego pieces and foot-long wires that would not connect together. The pieces were dark brown with old, scratched-up pieces of metal attached. I tried to help but I was very frustrated and just before I could share with him about his messy situation, I woke up.'*

I felt heavy and discouraged when I woke, but I did not know exactly why. The dream was so disjointed and abstract. It took me a while to put the pieces together and realize that it was a status quo dream. I did not see the man, but his world was disheveled and ineffective. Of course, the details in the dream were symbolic. They represented misguided aspects of his life and ministry. As I prayed, the Lord revealed who the man was, and I realized that the Lord had showed me his status quo. This was a picture of his life and ministry. I did not judge him before the dream or after it; instead I began to pray for him. I prayed that the Lord would help him organize with purpose so that his life and ministry would better hit the target.

# CHAPTER EIGHT

# Provision Dreams

## Dreams that Bring Peace

Different dreams bring peace. The peace of God may come to you through a glory dream, a teaching dream, a destiny dream or a provision dream. A provision dream is needed when there seems to be a shortage of God's benefits in your life. This can lead to anxiety, worry and fear. As one looks to the future they may have cause for concern because of uncertainty, threats, or a history of failure with no hope for change.

Such was the case with Hagar. She had been dismissed from Abraham's home and was forced into the desert with her young son, Ishmael. After their food and water ran out, Hagar set her son under a bush and went a good distance away because she did not want to see her son die. God intervened, and an angel spoke to her: *"Hagar...Do not be afraid... Lift the boy up and take him by the hand, for I will make him into a great nation." Then God opened her eyes and she saw a well of water. So she went and filled the skin with water and gave the boy a drink. Gen. 21:17-19*

Hagar had given up hope but the angel of the Lord spoke and promised her that God's provision would come. Peace replaced fear as her hopeless situation was turned around.

## Jacob's Dream

*"God spoke to Israel in a vision at night and said, 'Jacob...Do not be afraid to go down to Egypt, for I will make you a great nation there. I will go down to Egypt with you, and I will surely bring you back again.'...and Jacob and all his offspring went to Egypt." Gen. 46:2-4,6*

Jacob was afraid to leave the land of Canaan and move to Egypt. They had a good home where they were, and Egypt was a warrior nation set on conquering other peoples. He did not want to take his family into danger. God turned the situation around; he gave him a night vision or dream and told him that He would provide for him. The provision dream brought resolve and peace to an uncertain future.

Not every provision dream extinguishes fear, sometimes God is just letting you know that He has a great blessing to give you. Provision dreams will give you courage and faith so you have them for the future. You know in advance that God has taken care of things.

## My Provision Dreams

The Lord gave me an amazing provision dream. Years ago I was visiting in Canada, and I heard someone yell very loudly in my sleep. It was just one word, "LOOK!" I jumped out of bed and looked out the window but I saw nothing unusual. I asked the Lord what He wanted me to see. I opened my Bible but found no great revelation. Eventually, I laid down and fell asleep again.

Then, the provision dream came. I was sitting in a restaurant waiting for a meal, but it was taking a long time to come. I noticed the maitre'd standing nearby. He was dressed in a three piece Armani suit and I knew he was an angel. Finally, another angel came out of the kitchen. This one was a female and she carried a beautiful super-deluxe pizza on a pedestal tray. Suddenly, she tripped and the pizza went flying through the air in slow motion. Immediately, the tray flew out of the angel's hand and landed in the right spot to catch the pizza so it would not hit the floor. The pizza landed on the tray but now it was folded because it did not land perfectly.

Then, another angel placed a huge punch bowl full of orange sherbet ice cream down in front of me. I tried to make a joke with the angel. I said, "I see we are having dessert first." The angel did not laugh but stood up and walked away. Then, I woke up.

I felt the power of God all around me and I thanked the Lord for the dream. Then, the Lord told me that these were some of my provision angels. I was amazed, and I began thanking the Lord even more, but then I said to the Lord, "Father, I thought that angels were more professional. Why did the meal take so long to come from the kitchen, and why did that angel trip when she was bringing me the pizza?"

I heard the Lord say to my heart, "You did not see the demons hindering the food preparations in the kitchen nor did you see the demon that tripped the angel. I did not show them to you because I did not want you to focus on them. Know, however, that when your provision angels seem late or hindered, it is because of demonic interference."

## Another Provision Dream

I, along with my wife, Joy, and Jesse and Elizabeth Enns, are all pastors at Antioch International Church. In the past, we rented a facility that seated about two hundred people and once filled, our congregation stopped growing. We were on a quest to purchase a larger building. For two years, we searched and put offers on different facilities, but the banks would not lend us the mortgage money. After going around this mountain so many times, we put it to rest in the Lord's hands and quit looking. Months later, I had a dream and the message was clear; God was going to bless Antioch International Church with a great expansion. It would be so amazing that we would see it as a supernatural act of God.

I was so impacted by this provision dream that I shared it with the entire Church on Sunday morning. Then, within a month, a man who never heard me preach, offered us a huge facility on eighteen acres of land with two acres under roof. He also said he would sell it to us for half price and hold the mortgage.

If I had not received the provision dream, just weeks before, I would not have considered his offer. Now, however, I could not refuse it.

While the papers were being drawn up we realized our monthly costs would be four times our total monthly income from tithes and offerings. Still, we went forward. Within three months of receiving the dream, we were in the building worshipping the Lord. We have never put pressure on the members of our congregation to give money. It is not our way; we receive offerings, but we put our trust in God. More than eight years have passed since we moved into our church building. We have never missed paying a bill on time. We give all praise to God for His glorious provision. Provision dreams are powerful. I trust that you will experience many of them.

# CHAPTER NINE

# Warning Dreams

## Warning Dreams from God

From time to time, you might receive a terrifying dream that brings panic, heaviness and great concern. It is likely a warning dream. Its purpose is to make you aware of approaching evil, so you can prevent the attack. When you receive such a dream, do not think the evil will come to you or the person it is aimed at. In fact, the reason you received it is because God does not want it to happen in your life.

Recently, I received an email from a young lady who is a family friend. She asked for help because she had a dream that her father had died, and he is a young man. She thought that because she dreamed this, it was going to happen. Actually, the opposite is true, if she puts this matter to rest. I told her this was a warning dream and that she should ask the Lord how to pray so it would not happen. Then, I gave her specific guidance so she would know how to answer this warning properly.

Just imagine that every time you have an evil attack aimed at you, you could know of it before it happened. Imagine that you also received the ability to stop it. That is the purpose of a warning dream. The reason the dream is usually so dramatic is also a blessing. You may not like the experience, but because of its intensity, you pay serious attention to it.

## A Recent Warning Dream

About six months ago, I had a dream that my wife and I were driving in a rain storm. The storm ended, but there were branches on the road hindering our progress. We stopped the car, and I got out to move the branches.

I cleared the street but water began rushing down the road. I had to walk through the water to get back to the car. Suddenly, the road lowered toward a drain and I was in water up to my waist and its force pinned me down. I was alone in a frightening situation. Eventually, I managed to get back to the car and I woke up. It was a warning dream.

I prayed, but during the next few months, I went through some deep physical trials. It is what the Lord warned me about in my dream. First, I had a root canal that went seriously wrong and caused months of real difficulty. During that time my mouth would not open more than half an inch. Then, over the next season I got the Covid virus twice. I was in deep water and fighting a difficult battle.

Six months later, I am glad to say, that I recovered from all of those things. The Lord allowed them for a reason. Sometimes, ministers have to face difficult situations, so they are able to better empathize with the people they care for. The Lord gave me the warning dream so I would not be afraid when it happened. He wanted me to know that I would get though the deep water. The dream ended well and so have I.

Through the words of the prophet Agabus, Paul was warned that he would be incarcerated if he went to Jerusalem. He replied, *"I am ready not only to be bound, but also to die in Jerusalem for the name of the Lord Jesus." Acts 21:13*

Sometimes, a warning is just to prepare us for what we are about to face, but not to remove the danger.

## In the Bible

There are many warning dreams in the Bible; *"And having been warned in a dream not to go back to Herod, they returned to their country by another route." Mt. 2:12*

The Magi received a warning dream from God. They had met the Christ child and were ready to report his location to King Herod. They did not know that Herod wanted to kill the child but God warned them in a dream. As a result, they did not meet with the king, but went home another way. We are told the final message, but we did not receive the details of what happened in the dream. We can only guess. Perhaps, one of the Wise Men had a ter-rifying nightmare. He saw Herod's soldiers slashing children and one of them was Jesus. Perhaps, he woke up in a panic, covered in sweat. I am sure it was a power dream, and it affected him so much that the Magi were willing to disobey the king and leave the region immediately.

Scripture says, *"When Herod realized that he had been outwitted by the Magi, he was furious, and he gave orders to kill all the boys in Bethlehem..." Mt. 2:16*

This ruthless king would have killed the Wise Men, if he had caught them. He was furious. During the same week that God gave a dream to the Magi, He gave one to Joseph. *"When they had gone, an angel of the Lord appeared to Joseph in a dream. 'Get up.' he said, 'take the child and his mother and escape to Egypt. Stay there until I tell you, for Herod is going to search for the child to kill him.' So he got up, took the child and his mother during the night and left for Egypt." Mt. 2:13-14*

In the rush of the moment, the Wise Men did not retrace their steps to go back and tell Joseph of the warning dream. We do not know the reasons why. God, however, did not let Joseph and his family down. He was faithful to give him a warning dream and as soon as he woke, Joseph took Jesus and Mary and left for Egypt that night.

What about the other families who had infant boys living in the vicinity of Bethlehem? Maybe there were dozens of boys under two years of age who lived there. I am only guessing, but some could have received dreams or messages from God. Perhaps some children escaped because their parents listened to God and obeyed His word.

## Your Warning Dreams

If you are a believer and a dreamer, you will have warning dreams from time to time. They will be frightening and can possibly leave you in distress and panic. I have such dreams two or three times a year. Usually, after having a dream like that, I do not entertain fear or panic. I have learned that God is helping me with a warning; I thank Him and then I respond accordingly.

I know of people, however, who have such intense dreams every couple of weeks. These are dreams where you may be chased by a wild animal, find yourself drowning in water, face an evil spirit, run from a tsunami, shelter from a tornado or discover that you are fighting for your life against evil people. It is a warning and you should rebuke the evil menace in Jesus name. You should then ask the Lord what this attack signifies and deal with it accordingly.

If God is giving you warning dreams frequently, you need to draw closer to Him and get help closing spiritual doors that the devil is getting through. If you are a believer, the devil is not giving you those dreams, God is. He is exposing Satan's plan of attack against you. You may need to clean your house of ungodly things or have generational curses broken off of your life. If you are living a life of hidden sin or hypocrisy, you have open doors and you are a target. Getting your life and spiritual history right with God closes demonic doors, and in time, you will find that demons will attack you less. Freedom is the journey of the disciple. It is the life of the overcomer. A disciple's life is full of righteousness, peace and joy. May your dreams reflect such a walk with God.

# CHAPTER TEN

# Flushing Dreams

## Even These are from God

For a Christian, the worst kind of dreams are flushing dreams. There are two kinds of flushing dreams. One involves deep acts of sin that your flesh might actually enjoy. When your flesh is contemplating sin, demons will be there to tempt you, and provide opportunity for you to live out those temptations. These dreams, from God, reveal time-bomb temptations that are waiting for your moment of failure, success, or weakness, to explode and exploit you.

They involve such sins as sexual perversions, secret corruption, excessive greed, blood lust or narcissistic pride. If you give yourself to these vices, they will be destructive for you and hurt others around you. You should learn how to flush these temptations away. That is why God gives you flushing dreams. You have to renounce the activities in those dreams, realizing that these sins lead to death; *"for the wages of sin is death."* Rom. 6:23.

It is important for you to renounce these dreams. If you embrace the sin in them, you resist the work of the Holy Spirit in your life, and you tell the devil to bring it on. The dreams may be enjoyable for your flesh, and you may not want to renounce them, but you should, and if you are a disciple of Christ, you must. These dreams are designed to bring the fear of the Lord to you. *"The fear of the Lord is the beginning of wisdom."* Pro. 9:10

The Lord is giving you an opportunity to deal with a vulnerable area in your life. Even these flushing dreams are from Him. Scripture teaches us that apart from God, wickedness will be present. It says, *"The heart is deceitful above all things, and desperately wicked; who can know it?"* Jer. 17:9 NKJ

## Another Kind of Flushing Dream

The second kind of flushing dream is really awful. In such dreams, you see yourself involved in a sin that you consider to be unthinkable. You believe it would be impossible for you to involve yourself in that sin because you are not at all drawn to it. In fact, you are repulsed by the thought of that sin. Flushing dreams may contain some level of gross sexual perversion or very serious acts of corruption that are really extreme. When you wake from such dreams, you feel confused, depressed and dirty. It feels like you have been violated. You want to take a shower to wash the junk away. You wonder why you had such a dream, because the activity in the dream is not you. Now, you can't get these images out of your mind, and you might even be tormented by them.

You are right, in most cases, those activities do not represent your life, or your thinking, nevertheless, they represent the long-term plans of the devil that are aimed at you. He always overreaches. The enemy of your soul is scheming to destroy you and the Lord is uncovering Satan's plans. The devil wants to lead you in the paths of gross perversion, and his method is gradual and progressive.

Over the years, I have seen good Christians experiencing terrible situations: a close family member dies, they fall into sin, or they are slandered to the point of losing everything. When these things happen, some believers give up on their faith, and begin to walk in the way of sinners. In time, their lifestyle becomes sinful. If they do not turn from it, the sin becomes more perverse. They make excuses and embrace the sin with an, I don't care attitude. Then the devil will connect them with people who encourage dark perversions. Once people experiment and enter that dark world, they usually continue in that direction. They believe they have stepped over the line, and now they are beyond hope; they become self-destructive. Their darkness becomes so evil that lawlessness enters and they begin to defend their new lifestyle as if it were normal. By embracing the lie, they insist they have found their true identity. The devil's cunning has led them from godliness to depravity. The wickedness they saw in their flushing dream has become their reality.

It may seem impossible, but flushing dreams are extreme warnings of inner vulnerabilities. They flush out the schemes of the devil, so they are revealed and cut off before the slippery slope begins. When someone receives this kind of flushing dream, at the beginning, it is easy to rebuke and renounce. It is important that people do exactly that. The sin in those dreams does not represent who you are. Be sure to keep it that way.

## Flushing Dreams from God in the Bible

Flushing dreams are mentioned in the Bible, *"In a dream, in a vision of the night, when deep sleep falls on men as they slumber in their beds, he* [God] *may speak in their ears and terrify them with warnings, to turn man from wrongdoing and keep him from pride, to preserve his soul from the pit, his life from perishing by the sword."* Job 33:15-18

Notice that dreams and visions of the night are interchangeable terms. God will terrify people in their dreams to alert them of wrong paths or the schemes the devil is aiming at them. The purpose is to turn people from pride and wrongdoing. God watches over His children to preserve them, but they must do the righteous thing when they wake.

## What to Do

If you wake from a flushing dream, you should flush it away by renouncing it in Jesus' name, and confessing that you have no agreement with works of darkness. Then, you should rebuke the devil and he will flee from you. The devil's plans have been exposed, and that is a blessing. Even though the dream was nasty, you refuse it, renounce it, and rebuke the devil. That is a way for you to be saved from a path of sin and destruction. In most cases, the temptation will not even come because you have stopped the demons in their tracks and they will leave you. Even if a similar temptation comes in the near future, you will remember the dream and resist it with ease. You will be fortified, knowing the power you have in Christ and that the destructive plans of the devil have already been thwarted.

## In Everything Give Thanks

From my years of counseling people, I have come to the conclusion that everyone will experience a flushing dream. If flushing dreams are common place, you need to deal with your ungodly behavior, or the dark curses from your ancestry. For most Christians, flushing dreams are not experienced often. Nevertheless, do not think that because you had such a dream that, it is who you are. It is not who you are, but who you could be if you lose vision and cast off restraint.

Thank the Lord for watching over you to keep you. Just as you flush everything down a toilet, be sure to flush the perverse suggestions that appear in your flushing dreams. Flushing them away means they will be gone. It may need to happen on several occasions as the devil will want to return if he has opportunity. The path of the just, however, is like the sun that gets brighter and brighter until the full brightness at noon day. God is changing us.

# CHAPTER ELEVEN

# Apocalyptic Dreams

## Judgments are Coming

In the Bible, the book of Revelation, is also called The Apocalypse. Apocalypse means an unveiling or uncovering and it is specifically focused on judgments that will come to the earth at the end of the age. To my surprise, many people are having apocalyptic dreams, so I include it as one of the seven types of dreams. Apocalyptic visions and dreams are found throughout the Bible. They are in the books of Daniel, Ezekiel, and Revelation. The entire book of Revelation is a massive vision that was given to the apostle John while he was a prisoner on the Island of Patmos. Look at what he said. *"The horses and riders I saw in my vision looked like this: Their breast plates were fiery red, dark blue, and yellow as sulfur. The heads of the horses resembled the heads of lions, and out of their mouths came fire, smoke and sulfur. A third of mankind was killed by the plagues of fire, smoke and sulfur that came out of their mouths. The power of the horses was in their mouths and in their tails; for their tails were like snakes, having heads with which they inflict injury." Rev. 9:17-18* [emphasis mine]

These details are symbolic; they describe weapons of war. The fire, smoke and sulfur can be from cannon or gun fire from tanks and missile launchers. Two thousand years ago John was having a vision of wars in the end time. He had never seen modern weapons so his description of them is fitting. It is further proof that dreams and visions are not just a replay of things we have experienced in our lives.

My purpose in presenting these verses is to point out that John says these details are part of his vision. For a thorough interpretation of these verses and the rest of the book of Revelation, I recommend my book, <u>Unexpected Fire, A Powerful New Study on the Book of Revelation</u>.

There are twenty-two chapters in John's book of Revelation, all of which communicate an epic vision that the angel presented to him. This vision includes so many intricate parts that an entire book of the Bible was written just to record it.

## Nowadays

Nowadays, the word apocalypse means more than just "an uncovering" or "an unveiling". It is so aligned with the book of Revelation that it is identified with devastating wars, human initiated biological plagues, and catastrophic, natural disasters that cause excessive damage to the environment and people. These events are terrifying, unstoppable and sometimes inescapable. In apocalyptic dreams, people see tornadoes, earthquakes, volcanoes, hurricanes, devastating mud slides, tsunamis, plagues, famines, wars and mob violence.

## Apocalyptic Dreams

Apocalyptic dreams are warnings of trauma at a national or global scale. The natural disasters in these dreams will often symbolize geo-political attacks that are about to come from one nation against another. For example, a tsunami that destroys cities and towns, leaving death and ruin in its path, might have nothing to do with the ocean. It may refer to an invading army that occupies and crushes a neighboring nation. It could refer to an attack on the USA, like the traumas of 9/11, when Muslim extremists flew planes into the World Trade Center killing thousands. Someone might have had a dream showing a tidal wave rising out of the ocean and crashing into the World Trade Center.

## Also Futuristic

An apocalyptic dream may also refer to the great tribulation that will come upon the earth at the appointed time. Whether it refers to an event that is coming soon or one that will come in the distant future, the purpose is the same; it is a call from God for prayer.

When non-believers receive such dreams, it may cause the fear of God to come over them and draw them closer to the Lord. His purpose for people is to walk with Him and become part of His eternal plan. Sometimes, He will include them in His kingdom business even before they bow the knee and become disciples. After all, He created them for that journey and purpose.

## Prayer Partnership

Prophets, priests, ministers and disciples of Christ, are called to be ambassadors and partners with God. He always calls us to participate with Him in things that are beyond our natural abilities. An apocalyptic dream is one of those calls. The Lord shows us the trauma and devastation that is coming so we will intercede and release His compassion and mercy.

God tells us this in His Word, *"I looked for a man among them who would build up the wall and stand in the gap on behalf of the land so I would not have to destroy it, but I found none."* Eze. 22:30

In Ezekiel's time, God could not find a person to rebuild the broken walls of society and reform the sinful nation. Nor could He find someone to plead the case of the sinner so that His mercy might cover them. Today, He is looking for prayer partners, just as He was in Ezekiel's day. If people respond in the right way, much of God's judgment can be diverted and His mercy will be extended to many. Scripture says, *"Mercy triumphs over judgment."* *Jas. 2:13*

It is God's intention that His mercy will overtake judgment, however, there are conditions that must be met before this can happen. That is why reformation must come (building up a broken wall) and prayer partnership must flow from the hearts of His disciples (standing in the gap between God and the people).

He says, *"If my people, who are called by my name, will humble themselves and pray and seek my face and turn from their wicked ways, then I will hear from heaven, and I will forgive their sin and will heal their land."* *2Chr. 7:14*

## Our Response

A prophetic anointing is released when Christians receive apocalyptic dreams. Once disciples learn of the purpose for such dreams, they can step up and partner with the Lord. I know of many who do. They will pray because of the devastation they see in the dream. They will weep and cry out to the Lord for His mercy, for repentance to come to the lives of sinners, and for reformation to come so that evil will cease.

Some folks will even have an apocalyptic dream and be able to identify the nation involved and discern the sin and wickedness that is causing the judgment. Some of those people will not be people of prayer, but rather people called to bring political and cultural change. Dreams will help energize them to be reformers. God is at work with reformers as well as Intercessors.

A privilege and a trust is extended to disciples who receive apocalyptic dreams. May we understand our dreams and respond appropriately, so that we will see the purpose and provision of God for our lives and the communities around us.

# CHAPTER TWELVE

# Glory Dreams

## The Very Best

Glory dreams, are my favorite, because they include dreams and visions of Jesus, God's throne room, angels, bright shining light, miracles, flying, heavenly visits and even pictures of God's people in heaven.

Years ago, a family in our church had an eight year old daughter named Emily. She was hospitalized because of cancer. I went to visit her shortly before she passed away. Emily was full of faith and had the sweetest disposition. It was very difficult to sit at her bedside; she was bald due to the medicines the doctors had given, nevertheless, she was happy and full of life. During our conversation, Emily told me she was excited to share a dream with me from the night before. She said, "Pastor Peter, last night I went to heaven. I was with Jesus. Everything was bright and we were holding hands and walking together through a beautiful forest. There were colorful birds singing and flying everywhere. Jesus told me I would be coming to be with him soon."

I did everything to hold back my tears, as I agreed with her that she would soon be leaving us to go be with Jesus. I asked her to remember us when she got to heaven and to pray for Miss Joy, myself and our church when she was there. Emily promised that she would. She had received a glory dream and now, she was afraid of nothing. Emily was full of peace. I do not know why the Lord chose to take her home at such a young age, but I do know that her glory dream was God's provision. It was fantastic. At her funeral service, we had dozens of song birds in cages on the stage around the pulpit. We had large potted trees covering the platform and we celebrated the little one's life and thanked the Lord for her. Many people cried, but somehow, there was great joy in our hearts.

## Visions and Dreams of Glory

Several people in the Bible had visions and dreams of being in heaven. Isaiah, Ezekiel, Micaiah, Daniel, Stephen, Paul and John were taken to heaven in visions or dreams and at least eleven other individuals, plus the elders of Israel, saw the Lord in a vision. Here we see another example of the Lord giving a glory dream or vision to one of His children just before calling them home.

At the moment of his death, Stephen had a vision of God's throne room. Scripture says, *"But Stephen, full of the Holy Spirit, looked up to heaven and saw the glory of God, and Jesus standing at the right hand of God. 'Look,' he said, 'I see heaven open and the Son of Man standing at the right hand of God.'" Acts 7:55-56*

Jacob had an amazing glory dream. *"He had a dream in which he saw a stairway resting on the earth, with its top reaching to heaven, and the angels of God were ascending and descending on it. There above it stood the Lord, and he said; 'I am the Lord, the God of your father*

*Abraham and the God of Isaac. I will give you and your descendants the land on which you are lying'...When Jacob awoke from his sleep, he thought, 'Surely the Lord is in this place, and I was not aware of it..This is none other than the house of God'...He called the place Bethel...Then Jacob made a vow..." Gen. 28:12-13,16-17,19*

In Jacob's glory dream, he saw many angels, and more importantly, he saw the Lord. The Lord confirmed His blessing would rest on the people of Israel, and the land would be theirs as well. When Jacob woke up, he was filled with awe and wonder. He was so inspired that he called the place, "The House of God," he made a vow, rededicated his life, set up a memorial stone, and promised to pay his tithes to God.

## My Glory Dreams

I have had many glory dreams. In several, I have been with angels. I have also had a vision where God spoke to me in an audible voice telling me to plant a church in a specific city. I had another vision while I was serving as the director of Intercessors for Canada. It happened during a powerful Holy Spirit church meeting. I was on the floor, under the anointing, when the Lord brought me into a trance. He placed a map of the entire nation before me. Then, He enlarged each specific province until it zoomed out and filled the entire span of my vision. He told me to intercede and raise up intercessors for the nation and specifically for each of its provinces. His presence was so personal and powerful that I knew I was in the glory. I had received a glory vision.

## Glorious Flying

Flying in dreams is glorious and sometimes, I feel it is just for fun. I have flying dreams a few times every year, but I wish I had more of them. There are three different ways the Lord allows me to fly in dreams. One reminds me of the Superman style, where I just lift one arm above my head and suddenly I shoot up into the atmosphere, like a cannonball shot from a cannon. All I am missing is the cape.

The second kind of flying in my glory dreams happens when I stretch my arms out to the sides and I glide up into the sky like an eagle catching the thermal drafts. I zoom around buildings and over trees looking everywhere as the Lord directs me. Sometimes, I just fly around green hills and valleys observing the natural world and the beauty of God's creation. I choose the course I travel and the speed, as I see fit. The wind is blowing in my hair and I am exhilarated. It is absolutely delightful. Sometimes, I see groups of people in buildings or on the streets. I fly over and around them. They might be people that I know and the Lord shows me their needs and the situation they are in. I pray for them when I wake up.

In the third kind of flying dream I flap my arms and slowly rise off the earth. In some of those dreams I demonstrate to others how easy it is to fly. These dreams are so real that when I wake, I actually think I can fly. I have tried to flap my arms standing alongside my bed, but so far I have remained earthbound. There have been a few times when I find that an evil person is after me. I flap my arms to fly away, but I cannot seem to fly high enough or fast enough to escape. The evil person continues to come after me. In all of those dreams, I escape their grasps, but just barely. I realize that even in the glory, there is an evil that wants to bring me down. I pray accordingly when I awake.

## A Glorious Purpose

Although glory dreams often have an important message from the Lord, I am convinced that sometimes, they are given just because God wants to bless His children. I think this is especially true with flying dreams. Often, I wake from a glory dream with increased faith, a greater revelation of the Lord, and a fresh perspective of His power and grace.

After an exciting glory dream, I wake up refreshed, as if I have been sleeping for days. I feel amazing. It is like God has taken me to a deep-healing spa for a treatment. He has recreated me, equipped me and strengthened me for the task ahead. All I have to say is, "Lord, show me your glory, and let me fly again."

# CHAPTER THIRTEEN

# Destiny Dreams

## So Very Personal

Destiny dreams reveal God's calling and purpose for your life. They may focus on your assignments for a season, or some aspect of your life-long mission. They may describe the great person God sees you to be in the future, or some area where you are being called to step up into a higher level of purpose.

I have had many destiny dreams. Here are a few examples to show you what a destiny dream looks like. In some of the dreams, I saw myself preaching to one hundred thousand young people. In another, I was moving to the USA for ministry. In one amazing dream, I was high up, in the wheelhouse of a huge yacht, that somehow I owned. It was stationary, tied alongside a massive dock, inside a public marina. Suddenly, without any human involvement, it began to move forward. I watched from the wheelhouse as it broke through small boat slips, sending the wooden planks of the boardwalks flying in every direction. People who were swimming in the water, tried desperately to get out of the way. When the yacht had broken free of the marina, it gently turned and sailed out into the ocean.

For me, the meaning of the dream was clear. I would be moving from my present confinements to a larger place of ministry and purpose. Things might get a bit torn up during the transition, but the yacht was being directed by the Lord, and it was unstoppable. All of this happened as I moved from Canada to the United States.

In another dream, I saw myself in Africa with a room full of African people who were being taken advantage of. It seemed that no one was there to help them fight for justice. Suddenly, I stood up and said that I would stand with them, defend their cause, and help restore them to the blessings of God.

Throughout my life, my destiny dreams have led me to serve the Lord and I have taken specific steps in response to them. They have involved national ministry, as well as local church, equipping, impartation and direction. Many dreams helped keep my hand on the plow and stay the course even when circumstances did not look favorable and I felt like quitting.

## Destiny Dreams in the Bible

There are many destiny dreams in the Bible. Joseph, the son of Jacob, had two destiny dreams that got him into trouble. *"Joseph had a dream, and when he told it to his brothers, they hated him all the more. He said to them, "Listen, to this dream I had: We were binding sheaves of grain out in the field when suddenly my sheaf rose and stood upright, while your sheaves gathered around mine and bowed down to it.""* Gen. *37:5-7*

Sometimes, telling others of your destiny dreams is not wise. They can become jealous or, because they cannot imagine the destiny

God has for you, they might accuse you of being proud and will dislike you for it. They may distance themselves from you or even slander you and gossip about you. Be careful.

We read on in Joseph's story. *"His brothers said to him, 'Do you intend to reign over us? Will you actually rule us?' And they hated him all the more because of his dream and what he had said." Gen. 37:8*

God gave Joseph another dream to reinforce the message concerning his destiny. *"Then he had another dream, and he told it to his brothers. 'Listen,' he said, 'I had another dream, and this time the sun and moon and eleven stars were bowing down to me.' When he told his father as well as his brothers, his father rebuked him and said, 'What is this dream you had? Will your mother and I and your brothers actually come and bow down to the ground before you?' His brothers were jealous of him, but his father kept the matter in mind." Gen. 37:9-11*

Apparently, Joseph was a slow learner. Even after the rebuke he received for sharing the first dream, he continued to get himself in trouble, by sharing the second dream.

We discover later, however, that the details of the dreams came to pass. Joseph became

Prime Minister of Egypt and his parents and brothers did bow down before him. Joseph was not proud or arrogant toward his family and he always honored and blessed them. God had a destiny for Joseph to fulfill, and his dreams helped him hold the course during the rough years that led to his success.

When you receive a destiny dream, you know it was not of your own making; it came from God. You may therefore think it is okay to share it with others because they will know that you did not design the dream yourself. Somehow, this will not be the case. People may still put you in the dream design category, and blame you for its content.

## Paying Attention to Destiny Dreams

We have learned that we should be careful when sharing our destiny dreams because we can be seen as boastful and people might turn against us. Still, a destiny dream is extremely important, especially when the picture you receive goes way beyond the expectations you have of yourself.

When you see yourself, in a dream, doing something special, or being someone special, you should realize that you have received a destiny dream. You should humble yourself and give it to the Lord. Then watch to see how you might move into the important role depicted in your dream.

## Symbolic

Realize that your destiny dream is likely to be a riddle. The things you saw in the dream may not be literal but symbolic, like my dream of the yacht busting loose and moving me out into the ocean. It is obvious to me that symbols were involved. I do not think that I will ever own such a massive yacht, and I do not think that I will smash though a marina, busting the dock and sending everything flying. I do not think that the ocean in the dream is literal.

Likewise, the sheaves of wheat and the stars bowing down to Joseph, in his dreams, were not literal. They represented his brothers bowing down to him. The riddle of the dream was simple and everyone knew what it represented.

The dream I had, involving the yacht, was given to me more than twenty years ago. Since then, I have had some discouraging times when I felt like my life and ministry were at a standstill. The destiny dream told me that one day things would bust loose, in a good way, and nothing or no one, could stop it from happening. The Lord did move me, and the ministry forward. I did go from a stationary position, out into the expansive ocean of His government and purpose. I know that aspects of the dream have been fulfilled and more details will follow.

## Punchy and Powerful

What I just shared about the yacht was a lengthy destiny dream, but I have had some that were very short, but also powerful. While staying at a friend's house, during the days when I was visiting Derek Prince Ministries (DPM), to talk about my ministry there, I had a short punchy dream. I dreamt that I saw a car driving forward. Suddenly, the picture zoomed in on the car's front wheel. It was turning so fast that it began to look like it was slowly turning backwards. It reminded me of a prop on the front of a small airplane that looks like it is starting to turn backward at a certain point. Then, the Lord spoke to me, although not in an audible voice. He said, "Peter, You think things are moving slowly, but really, they are moving very fast."

I woke up and knew the Lord had been talking to me about the ministry and our move to the USA. Within a short period of time, things shifted and I was ministering in the United States, under the banner of DPM.

Since I entered the ministry as a young teen, the Lord has always sustained me with destiny dreams. I have come to rely on them as a major avenue of spiritual communication that He uses to help me on my journey.

# PART THREE

# Remembering, Interpreting, And Responding to Dreams

# CHAPTER FOURTEEN

# Remembering Dreams

## Careful How You Wake

If you are serious about hearing from God through dreams; He will speak to you. You should pray and ask Him to give you dreams before going to bed each night. The next challenge will be learning how to remember your dreams. Be mindful of how you wake each day. Try to wake up softly, with as gentle an alarm as possible. A loud disruptive alarm will usually drive your dreams away, and you will have a difficult time remembering them. I have a very quiet alarm on my phone. Almost every morning, however, I wake before my alarm sounds. Then, I turn it off, lie still and talk with the Lord. Sometimes, I know immediately what I have dreamed, and I move forward interpreting and responding. When it is a casual dream, I often remember it in bits and pieces. Then, as the moments pass, I remember more and I pray for the people in my dream. When I feel that I have apprehended enough, I get out of bed and begin my day. That initial process only takes a minute or two.

I am still quiet as I go about my morning routine, and I continue talking with God as more details surface in my memory. Although most of my dreams are not power dreams, every night, I discover some significance in them. Often, as I am quiet, I receive more revelation even an hour or more, later. I find myself thinking, "O my, that is why God gave me that dream," and I pray with deeper purpose as the day unfolds. I find that all of this happens without my day being interrupted or put on hold; it is just a normal part of my life. My dream-focus happens automatically, and for me, it is a dynamic aspect of my daily walk with the Lord.

## The Middle of the Night

You may be startled with a dream in the middle of the night, and you wake up. At that time, you will remember your dream, but you will be tired and want to roll over and continue sleeping. If you just received a power dream, you should write some of it down in a journal that you keep beside your bed. If you fail to do this, you will likely forget it by the morning. You will remember that you had a dream of significance, but realize that you have lost it. I think this is what happened to King Nebuchadnezzar. *The king asked Daniel (also called Belteshazzar), "Are you able to tell me what I saw in my dream and interpret it?" Dan. 2:26*

The king wanted to know what his dream was, and know its interpretation as well. He realized he had a powerful dream of great significance but could not remember it. I think he was too tired when he woke in the middle of the night, and he probably figured he would deal with it in the morning. He could have called for his scribes to write it down, and then gone back to sleep, but he failed to do so. When morning came, he could not remember his dream, and it haunted him.

## A Dream Journal

A dream journal is valuable because many dreams are about the future and some will even focus on destiny. When you review the journal months or years later, you will realize you had forgotten a good number of your dreams. You will be amazed at the dreams you had and how many have come to pass. You will recognize the realities of other dreams that are still unfolding. Upon reviewing my dream journal, I have found myself praying afresh for important matters that have not held my attention for a long time. This serves to fortify your faith and reinvigorate your spiritual focus. Without a dream journal, some important matters and guideposts in life may be lost. Use a dream journal, at least periodically.

When you write down part of your dream, in the middle of the night; do it in point form, and it will serve you well in the morning. As you read what you wrote, (even though it may look like chicken scratch) it will always help you remember the rest of the dream.

Another matter to consider is the importance of being a disciple of Christ. If you do not value your dreams (by writing down those you feel are significant) you communicate that either God does not speak in your dreams or that His words to you are not important. God speaks more readily to those who have ears to hear, and when He does, it may come in surprising ways.

## Remembering the Life-Changer Nights

I thought I had finished writing this chapter, but last night, in my dream, the Lord twice reminded me of the special nights. He further instructed me to include the subject in this chapter. I had meant to include it earlier, but it had slipped my mind, so I am glad that God speaks in dreams. He reminded me of the times when I had such powerful dreams that all sleep left me. I had to get out of bed, go to the living room, take my Bible in hand, and begin to pray. It happens about once a year. Those are such dramatic nights. The Lord pulls me into a proverbial wrestling match with Him. The dreams I have on those nights lead me to cry out, "Lord I desperately need your blessing." I confess my frailty and inadequacies to Him. I confess that the calling and task He has given me, is too great. He never releases me from the call, but puts things in perspective, so I am reminded that He is the Lord of my life. By the end of the night, His grace and peace always cover me. The process takes two or three hours and when it is finished, I am exhausted. When I return to my bed, I sleep like a rock. His momentary work, for my life, has been accomplished for now. I never forget those nights.

## Remembering Solid Ground

Some Christians do not appreciate the significance of their dreams. They do not think they are reliable and give no credence to them. Personally, I trust my dreams more than most prophetic words or ideas that I receive from other people.

The meaning of dreams should be tested because one's interpretation may be incorrect. Remembering your dreams and writing them down helps you understand they are from God. They are, as reliable, as any other word, the Lord speaks. That is of course, except for the Scriptures, which are always our final court of appeal for sound doctrine. We remember what we read in the Bible, and often remember the words of prophecy spoken over us, yet even power dreams, are usually forgotten.

Take your power dreams seriously and add them to the confirming words God gives for counsel and direction. If a word does not contradict the Bible, and is given in a couple of other ways, then it should be remembered and obeyed. It may be confirmed through a minister, signs and wonders, or dreams. When you receive confirmation, you can trust it to be God's word. Then respond to it with life-changing steps of faith.

# CHAPTER FIFTEEN

# Sharing Dreams with Others

## Severe Warnings

We have already mentioned the difficulty that Joseph faced when he shared his personal destiny dreams with his family. Sharing a dream that promotes yourself can make others jealous and cause them to distance themselves from you.

Besides the warning to be careful when sharing destiny dreams, the Lord warns about those who manipulate others through dreams.

I will record several places in the Bible where this warning is repeated so you grasp the importance of it:

"...*diviners see visions that lie; they tell dreams that are false, they give comfort in vain. There- fore my people wander like sheep oppressed for lack of a shepherd. 'My anger burns against the shepherds,'*" *Zec. 10:2* [emphasis mine]

"*If a prophet, or one who <u>foretells by dreams</u>, appears among you and announces to you a miraculous sign or wonder...and he says, 'Let us follow other gods'...you must not listen to the words of that prophet or dreamer. The Lord is testing you to find out whether you love him with all your heart...That prophet or dreamer must be put to death...You must purge the evil from among you.*" *Deut. 13:1,2,3,5* [emphasis mine]

Some charismatic people can influence oth- ers by using dreams, visions and miraculous signs. They use these phenomena to lead vul- nerable Christians away from God. That is a form of witchcraft.

In our society, we would never kill such an individual, as it is against the law. It is illegal, and it is outside of God's plan. In ancient times, however, witchcraft was recognized as being so serious that it carried the death penalty. We don't kill, but we should definitely separate ourselves from deceptive people who use dreams to manipulate others. We should find good shepherds that can protect and shield us from dream twisters.

*"Do not listen to what the prophets are prophesying to you; they fill you with false hopes. They <u>speak visions from their own minds</u>, not from the mouth of the Lord...I have heard what the prophets say who prophesy lies in my name. They say, '<u>I had a dream! I had a dream!</u>' How long will this continue in the hearts of these lying prophets, who prophesy the delusions of their own minds?"* Jer. 23:16 [emphasis mine]

The Bible encourages prophecy and tells us not to despise it (see 1Thes. 5:20-21). Nevertheless, we are instructed to judge it and receive confirmation so we will not be deceived or manipulated.

I will not write out the text, but here are a few more verses (for your study) that warn us about false people who use dreams to manipulate and control others (see Jer. 27:9, Jer. 29:8, Jude 1:8).

## If You Need Help

Sometimes you may need help interpreting your dreams. Go to someone you trust for godly answers in your life. The person you share your dream with should be spiritual, godly and have a gift of discernment and dream interpretation. They should be a person who does not manipulate or control others and should not be wounded or emotionally needy people.

In the Bible, God gave Joseph and Daniel a gift of dream interpretation. In most cases, a disciple of Christ will be taught by God to interpret their own dreams. But, there may be times when the Lord wants you to go to someone else for help. So you should find someone like a Joseph or a Daniel to help you.

## Be Careful

Just because something is misused does not disqualify the genuine article. Dreams from God are great and good interpretation is an amazing blessing.

I have met several folks, however, who came to our church from other groups where they were deceived and led astray. It messed them up, and took them off the path of God's goodness and grace. They were influenced by incorrect dream interpretation or other, so called, supernatural signs. I want to state it again; be careful who you share your dreams with. Even good intentioned people, can give false dream interpretation and it is dangerous, especially if those dreams are about your future. Huge deception comes from dream twisters.

As folks begin to minister to one another, they can share what they think is right, but be wrong. If they have deep needs for acceptance and approbation, and see rewards of gratitude coming from those to whom they minister, they may use dream interpretation with ulterior motives. Codependency may form among intercessors, worship teams, and in small group Bible studies. Faithful friendships are great and ministering to one another with the gifts of the Holy Spirit is fantastic, but be careful of manipulation and control. It is not wrong to share a dream with other people, but if you are looking for interpretation, go to the right person.

## Prophecy in Your Dream

The Lord may give you a message, in your dream, for another person, a family, or even for a group of people. It may be a warning dream, a dream for course correction, or one for encouragement. Sometimes, it is just a call for you to pray.

Other times you need to share this with the person or people it is directed toward. Then, like with all words of prophecy, you must wait on the Lord for His timing. There is a time for everything under the sun, but wrong timing can disqualify or discredit the effect of God's word. Some prophets in America, receive words from God in dreams, but share them prematurely, or assign them to a wrong date or season. When that happens, the word does not come to pass accordingly and the prophet is discredited.

Discernment is needed when prophesying a dream. Share the message, but do not always share the details of the dream. The Lord gave you the dream, and if you process it correctly, you will receive the interpretation. If you share every detail of a dream, others can attach their own interpretation to it, as if it were a free-for-all.

If the dream is straight forward, share the details. For example, if an angel, dressed in white, comes to you in a dream, and says that revival will come to America this year, and it will start in the North East. Then you can share all the details of the dream exactly as you received them.

If, however, in your dream you saw lightning and fast moving clouds over the Eastern Seaboard, with tornadoes spinning off up to the heavens, accompanied by an explosion of white light and rain falling like droplets of gold, you will need to be careful. If, in the dream, you felt the glory of the Lord and you woke knowing that you had just witnessed the work of angels and the release of a latter rain revival over the North East. And, on top of that you heard yourself repeating the calendar date of the year, you should share the message but not all the details.

At the appropriate time, you might share. *"I had a dream and God showed me powerful angels flying over the North East. They were releasing a latter day revival, like gold falling on the whole region. The Lord told me it would happen this year."*

Prophets share messages that the Lord gave them, but they do not always share how He showed it to them. If they share all the details, some people might see the clouds, tornadoes and lightning as judgment, or the rain of gold as economic blessings over the stock market. The Bible says: *"The spirits of the prophets are subject to the control of the prophets. For God is not a God of disorder but of peace." 1Cor. 14:32-33*

In other words, prophets must discern what to share and what not to share. God gives them authority so that His people will receive what they should, at the appropriate time.

## Share the Blessings

Be blessed with the dreams God sends; they are first of all, for you. They are designed to draw you closer to the Lord and help you move with Him in kingdom purpose. As He leads, share your dreams, at the right time, with the right people. Your dreams will be testimonies of God's amazing love, wisdom and power. If you had a teaching, provision, or glory dream, share it to increase the faith of others. The personal care, intimacy and blessings you received, because of your dreams, will help others grow in the knowledge of the greatness of God.

Sharing dreams may have another purpose. The Lord joins His children together in heartfelt fellowship. Sharing dreams with those close to us strengthens friendships and encourages genuine companionship. It is a vulnerability we give to special people in our lives. The treasures of the night are like uncut gems we gather from the earth and share with those we trust.

# CHAPTER SIXTEEN

# Interpreting Your Dreams

## Equipped for Dream Interpretation

Being able to correctly interpret your dreams is a sign of spiritual maturity. All of us are on a lifelong journey of discovery, and the more we walk with the Lord, the more we discover. He shows us Himself and who we are. He leads His disciples on a path of change while we are awake and asleep.

It is the task of all senior ministers to equip God's people for the work of the ministry (see

Eph.4:12-16). My goal, in writing this book, is to help equip you with dream interpretation. This will help you grow in Christ, become more mature, and connect you with God's purpose for your life.

Here are some steps to help you interpret dreams. First, remember the preliminary details that I shared with you in previous chapters. Then follow the list below.

1. Pray for God to give you dreams in the night.

2. Wake softly and lie still, to better discover your dreams.

3. A power dream will grab your attention. Work hard to understand it because it is important.

4. If the same dream comes to you a few times, pay close attention, it is important.

5. A casual dream may be mysterious, lie still, talk to God and review what you remember. Respond to what you understand and leave the rest with Him.

6. Always pray for people who appear in your dreams. Pray for their salvation, healing, and future.

7. Status quo dreams reveal disconnected details from your world. When you wake, you may feel heavy or confused because the dream is so abstract. God is showing you multiple aspects of life. Pray over what you understand, and leave the rest with Him.

8. Always trust the Lord with your dreams. Whatever is not of faith is sin. If you give Him everything, He will give you everything you need.

9. If you see yourself in your dream, the message, at least in part, is for you.

10. Always give thanks to the Lord for your dreams and for their interpretation, no matter how challenging they might be.

11. Ask the Lord what kind of dream you had. Was it a teaching, provision, warning, flushing, apocalyptic, glory or destiny dream?

12. Once you have determined what kind of dream you received, ask follow up questions. If you received a teaching dream, what were you being taught? If you had a warning dream, what were you being warned about?

13. Discern your emotions in the dream. Was the situation or the people good or evil? Your emotional discernment is accurate. This helps you respond appropriately.

14. Begin to solve the riddle of your dream. Start by recognizing the symbolism. In most cases, your car, for example, represents your life's journey; your ancestral home reveals the spiritual condition of your heritage, family or your life.

15. Continue to fill in all the blanks and line things up as best as you can. Your pastor may represent spiritual authority, an ocean may represent the government of God, deep, dark waters, or apocalyptic scenarios represent a demonic attack or judgment. Review the list of symbols given in chapter six.

16. Everyone has their own dream language and if you dream often, you will discover yours. For example; in my dreams, good, powerful lions are protection angels. So whenever they appear I immediately know what they are.

17. With an epic, story-dream, there may be some details you do not understand because they seem out of place. Their significance will come to you in time. If not, leave them on the shelf. Like with the scriptures, there are levels of revelation that unfold over time.

18. From time to time, you may receive a dream in black and white. If so, understand it is a dark warning dream.

19. Always test the message of your dream against the Scriptures. If God wants you to do something, it will not contradict His Word.

20. Judge yourself. In the process of interpreting your dreams, it is essential that you are honest and humble before the Lord. The Bible speaks of those who will be deceived because of their pride (see 2Thes. 2:10-11).

21. When you have a traumatic dream, pay attention to how it ended. It is likely a warning dream, and the ending is the most important part. Did you die? Were you being chased? Did the creature get you? Were you rescued? Did you live?

22. If the ending is good you should feel relieved. Thank the Lord. If you woke in trauma before the conclusion, pray for a good ending regarding the situation. You have been given an opportunity to make things right.

23. As you go about your day, continue to talk with the Lord about your dreams. More specifics and more interpretation will come.

24. As opportunity allows, write down your power dreams in a journal. The book will remember long after you forget.

25. If you had a power dream and need help with the interpretation, share it with a gifted person whom you trust. If they give you an interpretation, judge it. The Holy Spirit will confirm its validity or tell you when it is a misguided interpretation. Good intentions are not always accurate.

26. Ask the Lord if a dream is for you or for someone else? Is it a prophecy that should be shared? If so, follow the leading of the Holy Spirit so that you share it at the right time and in the right way.

## Gifts While You Sleep

Learning to interpret your dreams will reveal that they are gifts from God. Some may be disconcerting because they are warnings sent to expose the devil and give you what you need to fight your battles. Others, however, are delightful and will encourage and refresh you. Some may even show your future and release the secrets about God's purpose for your life.

I encourage you to start this journey if you have not already done so. Complete the circle of spiritual life. Walk with the Lord during the day and walk with Him through the night. He said that He would never leave you nor forsake you. Receive that in the literal sense and enjoy His presence always.

# CHAPTER SEVENTEEN

# Responding to Your Dreams

## Responding with Grace and Obedience

There is an old hymn that says, *"Trust and obey for there's no other way to be happy in Jesus but to trust and obey."* As God speaks, and His Word is confirmed, we must obey. We listen, trust and obey, and if we do, God speaks to us more. If we ignore His voice, we discover He speaks to us less. When we receive a message or interpretation of a dream, we should follow through with an obedient response.

After giving the following guidelines, I will review the seven types of dreams, and suggest a response you should take for each of them.

## General Responses to Dreams

1. Always give thanks for every dream you receive. Thank God for speaking to you.
2. Pray for all of the people in your dreams. Pray for their salvation, their healing and for them to have God's blessings in the future.
3. Many dreams are for intercessory purposes only. The Lord may reveal secret things about others that they would not be able to talk about. Pray and intercede for them and do not share those details with others; it is between you and the Lord.
4. Forgive those who have hurt you in life, especially when they show up in your dreams. Bless them, pray good things for them and love them as the Lord leads you.
5. Ask the Lord to help you understand and respond to your dreams appropriately.
6. Share your dreams with others who were in your dreams, but only if the Lord gives you a green light to do so.

7. Share prophetic words that you received in your dreams, at the appropriate time, and in the appropriate manner.
8. Share amazing encounters from your dreams as testimonies to inspire faith in others.

## Responses for the Seven Kinds of Dreams

Each kind of dream requires a different response. The Holy Spirit may tell you to do more than what I suggest. Your ability to hear God, how courageous you are to obey Him, what your calling is, and the authority you have in other people's lives, will determine what the Lord will ask you to do.

Some of God's people are prophets, pastors, intercessors or evangelists. Depending on your gifting, your response to dreams may differ. Here is what I recommend you do when you receive different kinds of dreams.

## 1. Responding to Teaching Dreams

A teaching dream may be for your personal education or to be shared with others. The first thing you do is give thanks for what He has shown you. Then, if it is a power dream, write it down in your dream journal.

Second, if you are a teacher, this writing will go beyond your prayer journal. It will be included in your teaching notes. You should work with what God has shown you; look up the theme in your Bible, read the Scriptures, and do a deeper study on the subject. It is likely that God is about to adjust your theology so pray, and be flexible.

Third, ask the Lord if and when you should teach what He has shown you. Sometimes, He gives revelation that lines up with Scripture, but it is so different from people's understanding, that you should not share it, at least at this time. Even when God releases you to share it, some Bible students may not shift their thinking. When you get the green light, always share it with humility.

## 2. Responding to Provision Dreams

A provision dream is given to reassure you of God's benefits and provisions for your life. Usually it is very specific and focuses on an area of need or blessing where He wants to demonstrate His care for you. Of course, the first thing you should do is thank Him.

Write the dream down in your journal. As you write, more details will likely come to mind. I remember one of the provision dreams I received many years ago. Recently I realized a new fulfillment for it; another detail has come to pass. I have received fresh revelation concerning it. At the time, I did not think that part of the dream was important, but now I see it that it is. I am amazed.

When you get a provision dream, begin to pray like Mary did, *"Let it be to me according to your word." Lk. 1:38 NKJ*

Ask the Lord what He wants you to do and take note of other people or places that you see in your dream. There may be things you will need to do as an act of faith, before you will see the full blessing of the dream unfold.

## 3. Responding to Warning Dreams

A warning dream is usually frightening or at least disconcerting. It is given to warn you of impending danger, or Satan's plans to attack someone whom the dream focuses on. When you wake from a warning dream, you could be traumatized and be in a state of panic. The reason this happens is to impact you with the seriousness of the matter. You received the dream, but that does not mean you are under attack. It may just be a warning of the devil's intentions. Your proper response may divert the attack.

When you wake, you should <u>immediately</u> rebuke the devil in the name of Jesus and renounce every evil intention aimed at you or the people in your dream. Be aggressive, and speak your rebuke with a strong voice. Resist the devil and he will flee from you. Do this, until you get the victory.

<u>The second step</u> is to call on the Lord for His covering and protection over your life and over those in your dream.

<u>The third step</u> is to renounce any place or doorway of darkness that may be open because it could allow such an attack. If you pray, the Lord will show you where the dark doors are.

<u>The fourth response</u> is to proclaim who you are in Christ. Declare verses of Scripture that focus on victory, protection and the provision of the Lord. These provisions, for example, include: God's compassionate care, deliverance, healing, angelic protection, long life, financial abundance, authority for ministry, favor in the

community, strength for your body and the light of the Lord to illuminate your path. With boldness, speak them over your life and family.

## 4. Responding to Flushing Dreams

A flushing dream shows you being involved in something very wrong. It may be a perverted act that you would never think of doing in real life. When you wake, you feel confused and dirty, like you need a bath. You should flush it out of your life. It differs from other warning dreams because it reveals a planned attack against your inner man. Other warning dreams reveal a planned attack against your body, your family or environment.

This may be an indication of a hidden secret in your life or an area where Satan plans to tempt you in the future, even though it is not in your thinking right now.

Your response is to rebuke and renounce such a vile attack. You should refuse it and command the devil to get behind you.

If you actually enjoy the dream, and do not want to flush it away, you need to repent and cry out to God for mercy and deliverance. He gave you this dream to uncover the dark intentions the devil has planned for you, so you may stop them. With the authority given to you in Jesus name, flush it down the drain.

## 5. Responding to Apocalyptic Dreams

Apocalyptic dreams involve events of terrible destruction and warn of great judgments that are coming. They may involve disasters like, tornadoes, hurricanes, tsunamis, earthquakes or devastating wars.

Our response is to pray and intercede for God's mercy to come to the people who will be affected by the demonic attack or judgment that is coming.

We may be assigned by God to preach repentance so God may forgive the people, heal the land, and divert the judgments that are coming.

Ask the Lord what needs to be done to divert the horrors that are coming. He sent Jonah to Nineveh and the people humbled themselves and repented. In response, God saved the city from annihilation.

We may also respond by praying for God's people who are in the path of this catastrophe. Ask the Lord to protect them and to shield them from all harm and danger. Ask Him to demonstrate His care for His people. He is compassionate and full of mercy.

## 6. Responding to Glory Dreams

A glory dream shows us a measure of God's glory. We are blessed to see the Lord, angels or His throne room. Glory dreams may also involve us doing the things that He and His angels do. For example, it may involve flying. Whatever we see in a glory dream will refresh us and increase our faith. We will feel like we have slept ten sleeps in one night.

When we wake up from a glory dream, we should thank God for His love and goodness toward us. We thank Him for His abiding presence in our lives. We thank Him for bringing us into His family and for making us His children. We thank Him for including us in His glory. Your faith will be strengthened and you will feel energized and emboldened to prophesy and proclaim His goodness. Let your blessings spill over with encouragement for others. Freely you have received, so freely give.

You may want to read the Psalms out loud and with a bold voice. *"Give thanks to the Lord for He is good." Ps. 107:1*

Praising the Lord and giving Him thanks will break down strongholds of darkness, set captives free and change the spiritual atmosphere around you. You will be emboldened after you experience a glory dream. You will be strengthened, excited and motivated into action. Be led by the Lord with your response.

## 7. Responding to Destiny Dreams

A destiny dream is a message from the Lord that highlights His purpose for our lives. If we are a humble disciple of Christ, a destiny dream will reveal more about us than what we expect.

After thanking the Lord, our response to a destiny dream should first and foremost be one of humility. Scripture says, *"God resists the proud but gives grace to the humble." 1Pe. 5:5*

We should only speak of our destiny dreams to: close family members, friends, co-workers or to a larger group, when we are able to do it in a guarded way. Even then, we risk being misunderstood.

We give thanks to God for showing us part of our destiny. Our destiny will always be a small part of His huge plan, and we are honored to be a part of it.

A destiny dream is given to encourage and help us hold the course, as we face challenges along the way. When we are able to see a part of our destiny, we can cooperate with the Lord as He unfolds it. We receive faith to believe in our future.

There will be a time when we must step out and cooperate with our destiny dreams by exercising faith. I have known of people who refused their destiny because they were afraid to step out. Others refused it, because they had a grandiose, money making venture before them.

Derek Prince, my grandfather, used to say, *"There are two things that are never convenient, judgment day and the call of God on your life."*

Even though our destiny is amazing, it will be expensive. It will cost us the focus and energy of our lives and it will not be easy. In the end, it will be rewarding, but along the way it will mean a lot of hard work. All vision boils down to hard work.

If you are a good disciple, you will embrace the destiny the Lord has for you. Respond with thanksgiving, faith, obedience and expectation. The results will be amazing.

# CHAPTER EIGHTEEN

# Discipleship, Healing, Destiny

## Purpose

One reason God gives dreams to His children is for their healing. Another is for the procurement of their destiny. If you recognize the kind of dreams you have, and respond appropriately, supernatural change will follow. God will disciple you through dreams and He will be completely thorough in the process. This doesn't happen overnight, but throughout your life.

All of us come to the Lord with negative baggage, but His plan is to remove it. Jesus died to eradicate ungodliness from our lives and dismiss any curses that have come on us because of the sins of our ancestors. The debt of sin was fully paid for at the cross.

Christians are forgiven, but living in perfection is a different matter. That comes through a process of God working in us over time. The process is called sanctification. I spoke of this earlier but I am restating it to set up the theme of discipleship through dreams. Sanctification literally means, being made holy. Through it; we are forgiven, delivered from darkness, renewed in our thinking, and transformed behaviorally.

The changes we encounter are radical and wonderful. They may include deliverance from demons and the removal of strongholds that accompany them. We expect our personality to change to be more Christ-like. The shift is not just in our inner man; our lifestyle and activities will be different as we follow the Lordship of Jesus and submit to His governmental rule. If we obey the Lord with total abandonment, we will no longer live to serve ourselves, but Him. It means we extend more kindness and generosity to those around us and we care for the souls of our neighbors. We pray and exercise supernatural gifts as the Holy Spirit enables us. Ultimately, we heal the sick, cast out demons, save souls, and change the spiritual atmosphere in our world. We experience God's abiding presence and He gives us wisdom, righteousness, power and love.

## Especially in Dreams

This process of sanctification and discipleship can flow from the dreams God gives us. If we cooperate, He will disciple us in our sleep as well as in our waking hours.

Many Christians are going to counselors for help with their inner struggles. Usually, inner healing takes time and may require the direction of a counselor, who knows how to activate the provisions of the Lord in someone's life. If counselors do not understand the work of the Holy Spirit, they may diagnose the problems, refer to them in technical terms, get people talking about their situation and prescribe pharmaceutical drugs, but still not bring about transformative change. Skillful, God focused counselors can add the missing ingredient; the transformative anointing that comes from the

Holy Spirit, through the release of faith, for-giveness, obedience and prayer.

## The Discipleship Process

The same help that a godly counselor may pro-vide, over many sessions, can flow from dream encounters. It is not the dreams that heal, but your response to them. A person's appropri-ate and immediate proclamations ward off the devil, and connect them to God's blessings. The ongoing multi-focused encounters will lead a person to sanctification.

If you pray for everyone in your dreams, for example, you will soon discover that you are praying a lot more. You will tend to walk in the presence of the Lord more, because you are constantly talking with Him about your dreams. The mystery of dreams will draw you to seek the Lord and, through seeking, you will find Him and become more spiritual.

If you are paying attention, unusual insights and prophetic words will be given to you in dreams. The Lord will teach you through teaching dreams and warn you through warn-ing dreams. He will show you His provision in provision dreams and you will have greater faith. When He gives you an apocalyptic dream, you will learn how to pray beyond the realm of your own existence. Even deliverance will come to you as you rebuke and renounce the devil after receiving a flushing dream.

God will engage you with the prophetic gift, discernment, faith and intercession. He will call you up to the destiny He has planned for you and give you words He wants you to share with others. The two things He is after through dream encounters are your healing and destiny.

## Specific Training

With <u>teaching dreams</u>, you thank God, interpret and understand the teaching. You put what you have learned into practice and your perspective and lifestyle changes. <u>That is how God disciples you.</u>

With <u>warning or flushing dreams</u>, you rebuke the devil, renouncing witchcraft and all evil. That will drive the devil from you and deliver you from any vestige of demonic activity. You will rebuke sickness and command healing to come, in Jesus name. You will be led to close dark doors, even those that were opened by your ancestors. Over time, more cleansing and deliverance will follow. <u>That is how God disciples you</u>.

<u>Provision and glory dreams</u> increase your faith exponentially. You are refreshed by the presence of the Lord and witness His care and protection over your life. When you wake, you thank the Lord and claim the blessings He showed you in the dream. You pray, prophesy, and declare the details and they will come to pass. <u>That is how the Lord disciples you</u>.

<u>Destiny dreams</u> wow you. You ponder over them and hold them in your heart as treasures. You speak acceptance of them to the Lord, and come into agreement with His plan.

There will be a new expectancy in your life, as you watch the fingerprints of God lead you to your destiny. You take steps of faith because of what He showed you in your dreams. You are not surprised, but you are thankful. You actually step into your destiny with humility because you know God has opened doors for you. <u>That is how the Lord disciples you</u>.

Even <u>apocalyptic dreams</u> work the purposes of God into your life. Through them, you carry the burden of His heart for humanity and you intercede for people to receive protection, compassion and mercy. You understand the resolve of God, and the pathways of man. You witness miracles and recognize God's sovereignty. <u>That is how the Lord disciples you</u>.

## The Dream Disciple

The Lord disciples His people through every aspect of life. It comes through the study of Scripture, inner promptings of the Holy Spirit, mentors and teachers, the school of hard knocks, and testimonies from the people of God.

As described, discipleship also comes through a lifetime of dream encounters. The purpose of dreams is to change you, in every possible way, to be a kingdom of God person. He knows what you need, and will give you dream encounters to help facilitate your complete healing, and the fulfillment of your destiny. The Lord will leave no stone unturned. You may think some dreams are too nasty, inappropriate or unnecessary, but God knows what to do to complete your journey. In life, you may resist correction, insight or spiritual realities, but through dreams they are all brought to the surface. Dreams may in fact be the most thorough and complete activity of discipleship in your life. Knowing this makes all the difference, so I encourage you: appreciate your dreams.

# CHAPTER NINETEEN

# Praying for a Deeper Dream Life

## Embracing Your Dream Life

If you want more of God in your life, the process may involve embracing dreams. As we bring this study to a close, I want to lead you in a prayer of dedication. I want this to be a prayer of total surrender to the Lord Jesus Christ and a prayer that embraces everything that God has for you. That includes a request to the Most High for dreams, interpretation of dreams and the follow through of obedient service.

Please rise to your feet and put your hand on your heart as if you were about to say the pledge of allegiance. Then speak these words out loud, before God, and mean them with all of your heart.

*"Heavenly Father, I come before you in the powerful name of Jesus. Thank you for creating me for your kingdom purpose.*

*Forgive me for all of my sins and wash my soul and spirit clean, by the sacrifice of Jesus' blood on the cross. Today, I dedicate my life to you and to your service. Fill me with your Holy Spirit and open my spiritual ears that I may always hear your voice. Lord, I ask that you speak to me during the days and also through the nights. Remove the blockages that hinder my spiritual hearing so I will be able to hear from you at all times. I surrender every part of my being and body to you. My body shall be a temple of the Holy Spirit, my mind shall be focused on obeying you, my tongue shall speak and sing of your praises, and my hands shall serve you with acts of kindness, compassion and generosity.*

*Lord, I ask specifically that you speak to me in dreams, visions and with revelations. Help me to be in step with you so I may know your voice and interpret my dreams accurately. Thank you for all that you have done for me so far, but I ask that you draw me closer to you so I might recognize your presence with me at all times. Heavenly Father, let me sleep in your presence and wake in your presence. Let all my dreams be governed by you and may they lead me forward in your kingdom. My days and nights are yours. Let them be used for your glory throughout eternity. Amen."*

## OTHER TITLES BY DR. PETER WYNS

Raising our Children for God:
A Generational Study

The Kingdom Coalition Manifesto:
Expanded Edition

Understanding God's Great Plan: A Jewish,
Christian, Bible Perspective

Blessings or Curses for the Next Generation

Israel's Coming Revival

America in the Last Days: The Jonah Nation

Unexpected Fire: A Powerful new study
on the Book of Revelation

Poetic Fire: Understanding the Book
of Revelation (put to Poetry)

The Powerful Little No Rapture Book:
What the Bible says about a Rapture

Proclamations for Life: Changing Your
Life by Declaring God's Word

Prayer that Hits the Target

Fighting Death and Other Desperate Battles

Great Reward for Kids #1:
Spiritual Studies for Children

Great Reward for Kids #2:
Spiritual Studies for Children

Great Reward for Kids #3:
Spiritual Studies for Children

Chronicles of Righteousness Volume One:
Fifty Powerful Sermons to Help
Equip God's People

Chronicles of Righteousness Volume Two:
Fifty Powerful Sermons to Help
Equip God's People

Chronicles of Righteousness Volume Three:
Fifty Powerful Sermons to Help
Equip God's People

To order, visit www.peterwyns.com
or call 803-324-0739